EASY GUITAR WITH NOTES & TAB

The Big Book of Nursery Rhymes & Children's Songs

ISBN 978-1-4584-2288-0

Music Sales America

Exclusively Distributed By

HAL•LEONARD® CORPORATION

7777 W. Bluemound Rd. P.O. Box 13819 Milwaukee, WI 53213

Visit Hal Leonard Online at
www.halleonard.com

Contents

STRUM AND PICK PATTERNS

This chart contains the suggested strum and pick patterns that are referred to by number at the beginning of each song in this book. The symbols ⊓ and ∨ in the strum patterns refer to down and up strokes, respectively. The letters in the pick patterns indicate which right-hand fingers play which strings.

p = thumb
i = index finger
m = middle finger
a = ring finger

For example; Pick Pattern 2
is played: thumb - index - middle - ring

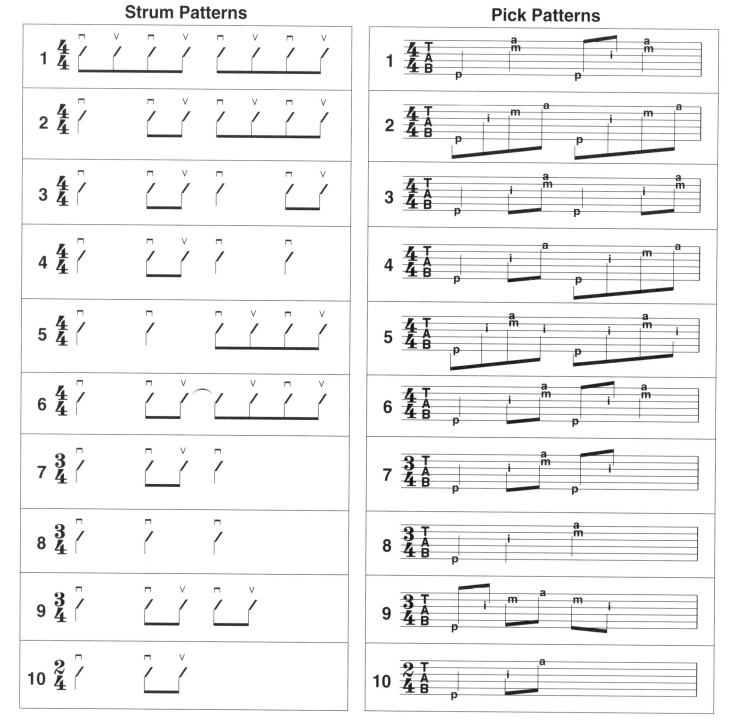

You can use the 3/4 Strum and Pick Patterns in songs written in compound meter (6/8, 9/8, 12/8, etc.).
For example, you can accompany a song in 6/8 by playing the 3/4 pattern twice in each measure.
The 4/4 Strum and Pick Patterns can be used for songs written in cut time (¢) by doubling the note time values in the patterns. Each pattern would therefore last two measures in cut time.

A-Hunting We Will Go

Traditional

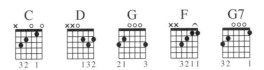

Strum Pattern: 4
Pick Pattern: 5

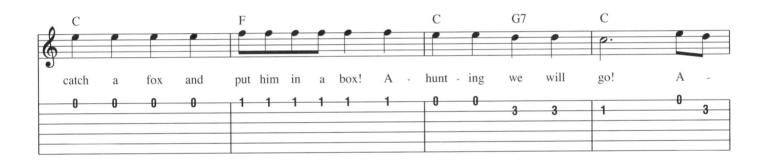

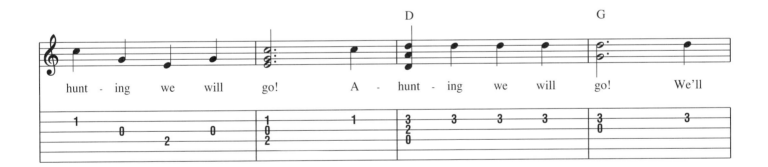

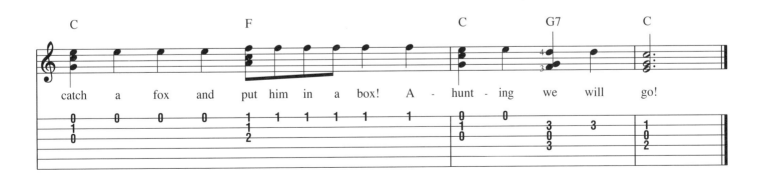

A-Tisket A-Tasket

Traditional

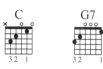

Strum Pattern: 10
Pick Pattern: 10

Moderately

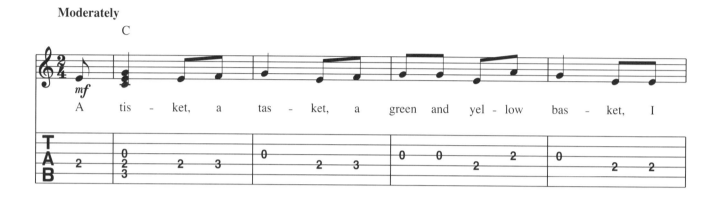

A tis - ket, a tas - ket, a green and yel - low bas - ket, I

wrote a let - ter to my love and on the way I dropped it, I

dropped it, I dropped it, and on the way I dropped, it, a

lit - tle boy (girl) picked it up and put it in his (her) pock - et.

Alice the Camel

Traditional

Strum Pattern: 3
Pick Pattern: 3

Verse
Moderately

1. Al - ice the ca - mel has five humps. Al - ice the ca - mel has
2. - 6. *See additional lyrics*

five humps. Al - ice the ca - mel has five humps so

go, Al - ice, go. Boom, boom, boom. Al - ice is a horse!

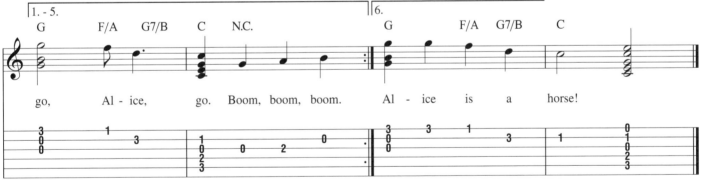

Additional Lyrics

2. Alice the camel has four humps.
Alice the camel has four humps.
Alice the camel has four humps
So go, Alice, go.
Boom, boom, boom.

3. Alice the camel has three humps.
Alice the camel has three humps.
Alice the camel has three humps
So go, Alice, go.
Boom, boom, boom.

4. Alice the camel has two humps. *etc.*

5. Alice the camel has one hump. *etc.*

6. Alice the camel has no humps.
Alice the camel has no humps.
Alice the camel has no humps
So Alice is a horse!

All the Pretty Little Horses

Southeastern American Folksong

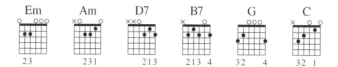

Strum Pattern: 4
Pick Pattern: 5

Verse
Moderately

1. Hush - a - bye, don't you cry, go to sleep - y, lit - tle
   When you wake you shall have all the pret - ty lit - tle

2., 3. *See additional lyrics*

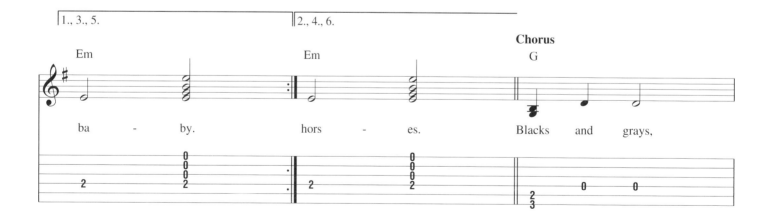

ba - by. hors - es. Blacks and grays,

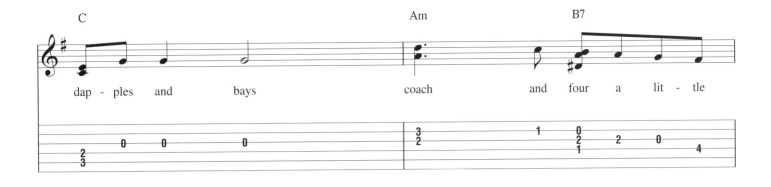

dap - ples and bays coach and four a lit - tle

hors - es. Hush - a - bye, don't you cry,

3rd time, To Coda

D.C. al Coda
(take repeats)

$\oplus$ **Coda**

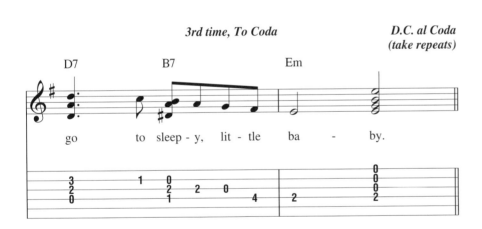

go to sleep - y, lit - tle ba - by.

ba - by.

Additional Lyrics

2. Hush-a-bye, don't you cry,
   Go to sleepy, little baby.
   Way down yonder in the meadow
   Lies a poor little lambie.

3. The bees and the butterflies pecking out its eyes,
   The poor little thing cried, "Mammy."
   Hush-a-bye, don't you cry,
   Go to sleepy, little baby.

Alouette

Traditional

Strum Pattern: 10
Pick Pattern: 10

Chorus
Moderately

mf A - lou - et - te, gen - tille A - lou - et - te,

A - lou - et - te, je te plu - me - rai.

Verse

1., 7. Je te plu - me - rai la tête, je te plu - me - rai la tête,
2. – 6. *See additional lyrics*

Play 7 times

Outro-Chorus

Additional Lyrics

2) le bec
3) le cou
4) les jambes
5) les pieds
6) les pattes

Animal Fair

American Folksong

Strum Pattern: 8
Pick Pattern: 8

Lively

I went to the an-i-mal fair, _____ the birds and beasts were there. _____ The

big ba-boon, by the light of the moon, was comb-ing his au-burn hair. _____ The

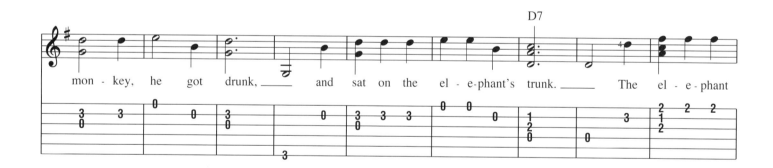

mon-key, he got drunk, _____ and sat on the el-e-phant's trunk. _____ The el-e-phant

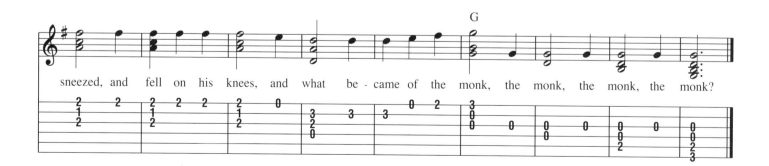

sneezed, and fell on his knees, and what be-came of the monk, the monk, the monk, the monk?

Baa Baa Black Sheep

Traditional

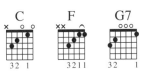

Strum Pattern: 10
Pick Pattern: 10

Moderately

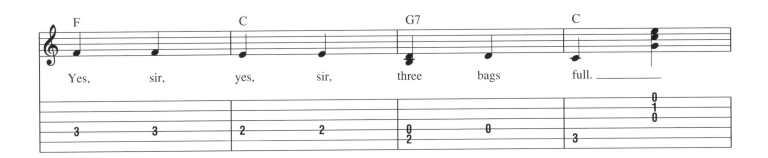

Baa, baa, black sheep have you an-y wool?

Yes, sir, yes, sir, three bags full. _____

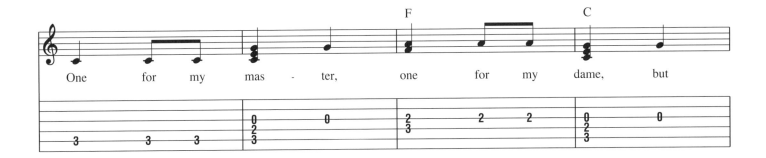

One for my mas-ter, one for my dame, but

none for the lit-tle boy who cries in the lane. _____

The Ants Came Marching

Traditional

Strum Pattern: 8
Pick Pattern: 8

Verse
Moderately, in 2

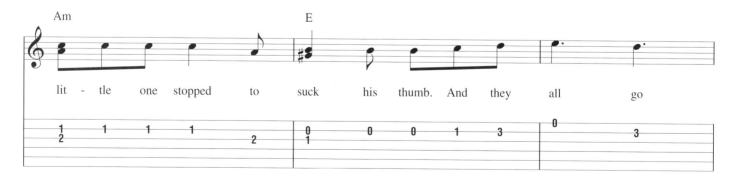

Additional Lyrics

2. The ants came marching two by two, hurrah! Hurrah!
   The ants came marching two by two, hurrah! Hurrah!
   The ants came marching two by two,
   The little one stopped to tie his shoe,
   And they all go marching down to the ground
   To get out of the rain. Boom, boom, boom.

3. The ants came marching three by three, hurrah! Hurrah!
   The ants came marching three by three, hurrah! Hurrah!
   The ants came marching three by three,
   The little one stopped to climb a tree,
   And they all go marching down to the ground
   To get out of the rain. Boom, boom, boom.

4. The ants came marching four by four, hurrah! Hurrah!
   The ants came marching four by four, hurrah! Hurrah!
   The ants came marching four by four,
   The little one stopped to shut the door,
   And they all go marching down to the ground
   To get out of the rain. Boom, boom, boom.

5. The ants came marching five by five, hurrah! Hurrah!
   The ants came marching five by five, hurrah! Hurrah!
   The ants came marching five by five,
   The little one stopped to take a dive,
   And they all go marching down to the ground
   To get out of the rain. Boom, boom, boom.

6. The ants came marching six by six, hurrah! Hurrah!
   The ants came marching six by six, hurrah! Hurrah!
   The ants came marching six by six,
   The little one stopped to pick up sticks,
   And they all go marching down to the ground
   To get out of the rain. Boom, boom, boom.

7. The ants came marching seven by seven, hurrah! Hurrah!
   The ants came marching seven by seven, hurrah! Hurrah!
   The ants came marching seven by seven,
   The little one stopped to pray to heaven,
   And they all go marching down to the ground
   To get out of the rain. Boom, boom, boom.

8. The ants came marching eight by eight, hurrah! Hurrah!
   The ants came marching eight by eight, hurrah! Hurrah!
   The ants came marching eight by eight,
   The little one stopped to shut the gate,
   And they all go marching down to the ground
   To get out of the rain. Boom, boom, boom.

9. The ants came marching nine by nine, hurrah! Hurrah!
   The ants came marching nine by nine, hurrah! Hurrah!
   The ants came marching nine by nine,
   The little one stopped to check the time,
   And they all go marching down to the ground
   To get out of the rain. Boom, boom, boom.

10. The ants came marching ten by ten, hurrah! Hurrah!
    The ants came marching ten by ten, hurrah! Hurrah!
    The ants came marching ten by ten,
    The little one stopped to say, "The end,"
    And they all go marching down to the ground
    To get out of the rain. Boom, boom!

Baby Bumble Bee

Traditional

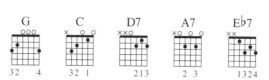

Strum Pattern: 3
Pick Pattern: 3

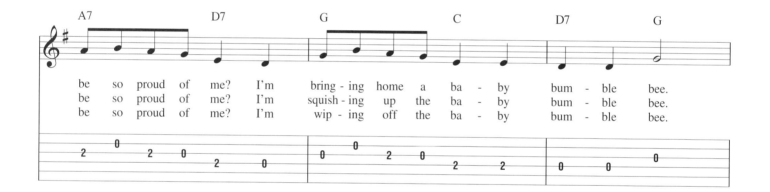

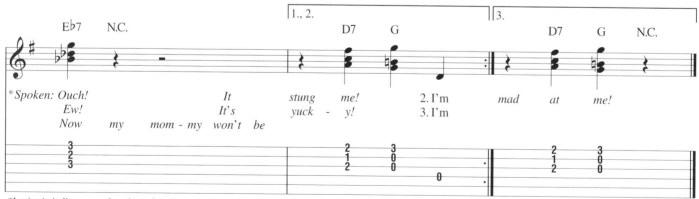

*Lyrics in italics are spoken throughout.

Barnyard Song

Traditional

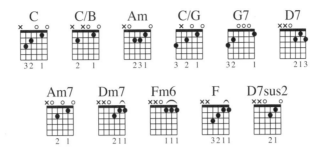

Strum Pattern: 7, 8
Pick Pattern: 7, 8

Verse
Moderately fast

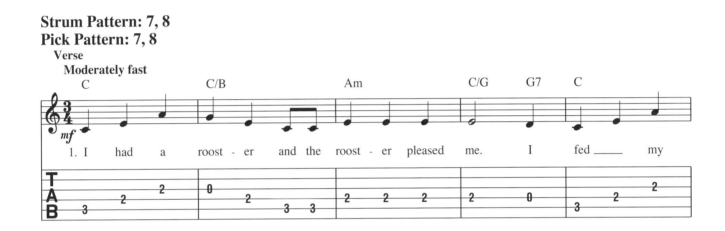

1. I had a roost-er and the roost-er pleased me. I fed ___ my

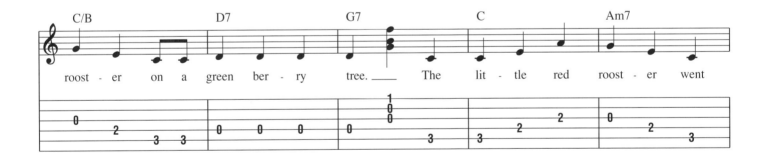

roost-er on a green ber-ry tree. ___ The lit-tle red roost-er went

"cock-a-doo-dle doo, dee doo-dle-dee, doo-dle-dee, doo-dle-dee doo." ___

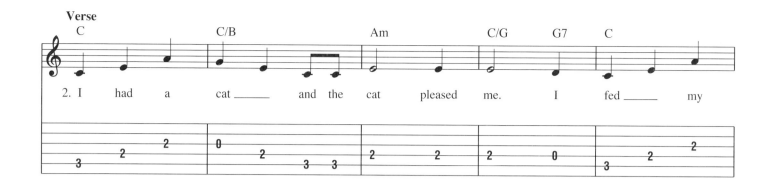

Verse

2. I had a cat _____ and the cat pleased me. I fed _____ my

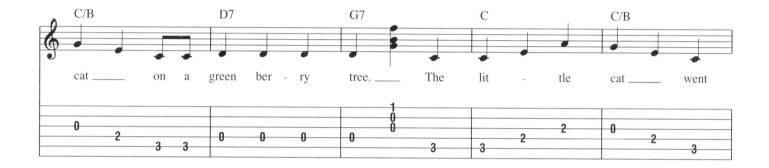

cat _____ on a green ber - ry tree. _____ The lit - tle cat _____ went

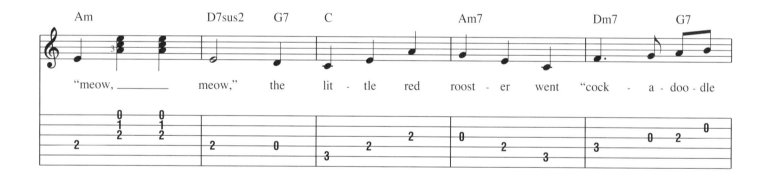

"meow, _____ meow," the lit - tle red roost - er went "cock - a - doo - dle

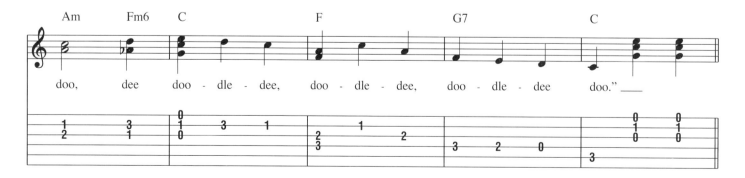

doo, dee doo - dle - dee, doo - dle - dee, doo - dle - dee doo." _____

3. I had a pig ____ and the pig pleased me. I fed ____ my
4., 5. *See additional lyrics*

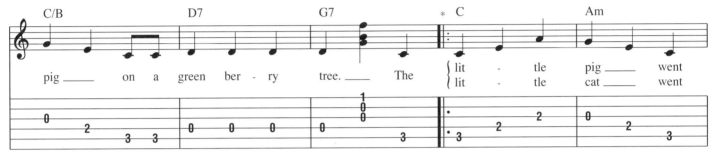

pig ____ on a green ber - ry tree. ____ The { lit - tle pig ____ went
{ lit - tle cat ____ went

*Verses 4. and 5.: repeat as needed for each animal

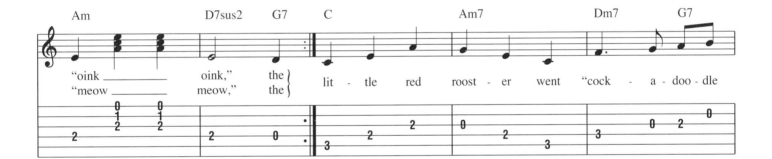

"oink _____ oink," the { lit - tle red roost - er went "cock - a - doo - dle
"meow _____ meow," the {

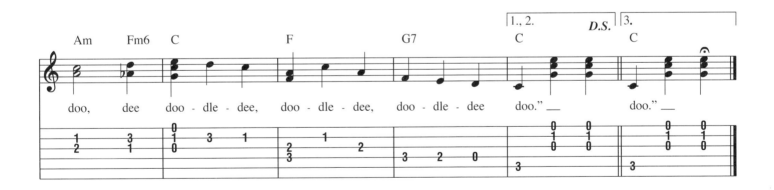

1., 2.   *D.S.*   3.

doo, dee doo - dle - dee, doo - dle - dee, doo - dle - dee doo." ____ doo." ____

Additional Lyrics

4. I had a cow and the cow pleased me.
   I fed my cow on a green berry tree.
   The little cow went "moo, moo."
   The little pig went "oink, oink."
   The little cat went "meow, meow."
   The little red rooster went "cock-a-doodle-doo,
   Dee doodle-dee, doodle-dee, doodle-dee doo."

5. I had a baby and the baby pleased me.
   I fed my baby on a green berry tree.
   The little baby went "waah, waah."
   The little cow went "moo, moo."
   The little pig went "oink, oink."
   The little cat went "meow, meow."
   The little red rooster went "cock-a-doodle-doo,
   Dee doodle-dee, doodle-dee, doodle-dee doo."

The Bear Went Over the Mountain

Traditional

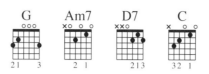

Strum Pattern: 8
Pick Pattern: 8

Verse
Brightly

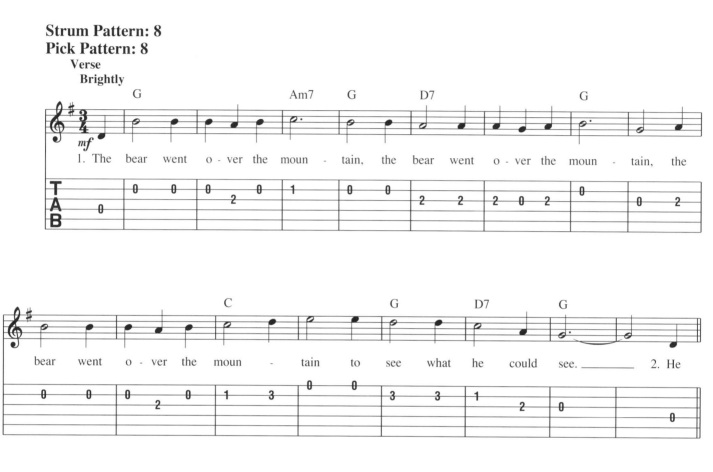

1. The bear went o-ver the moun-tain, the bear went o-ver the moun-tain, the

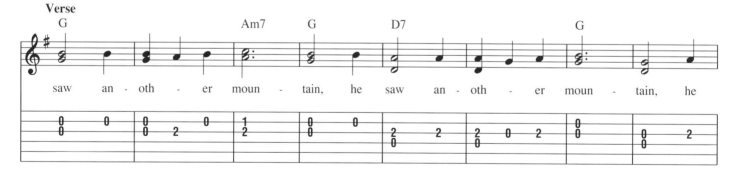

bear went o-ver the moun-tain to see what he could see. ___ 2. He

Verse

saw an-oth-er moun-tain, he saw an-oth-er moun-tain, he

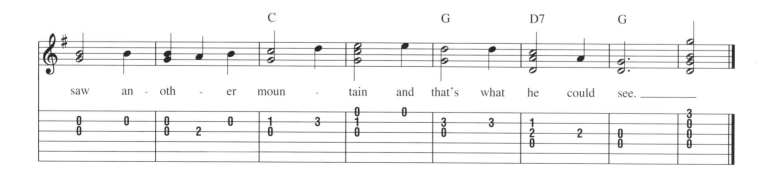

saw an-oth-er moun-tain and that's what he could see. ___

Bye, Baby Bunting

Traditional

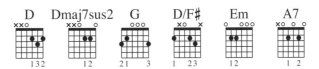

Strum Pattern: 7
Pick Pattern: 7

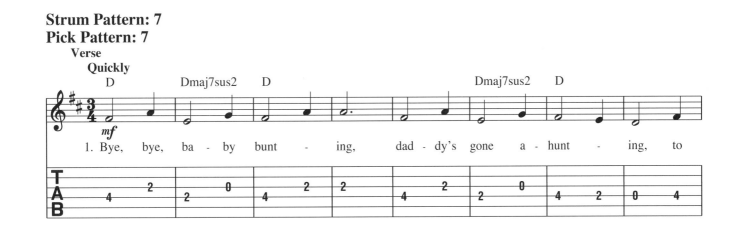

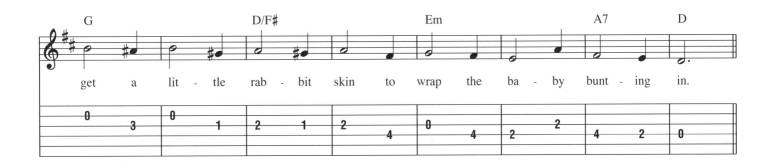

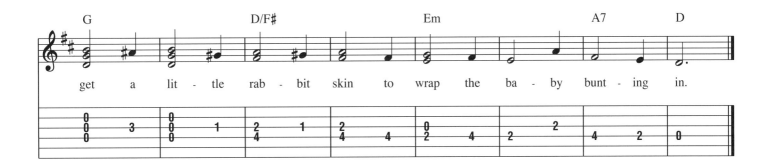

Blowing Bubbles

Traditional

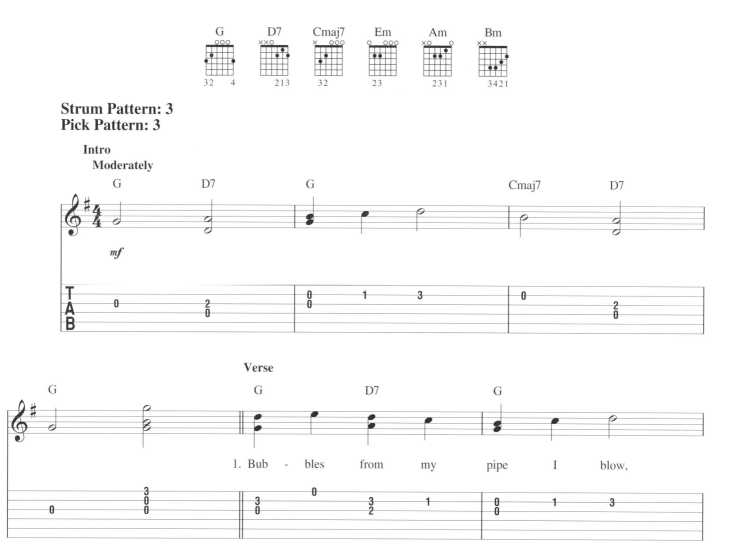

Strum Pattern: 3
Pick Pattern: 3

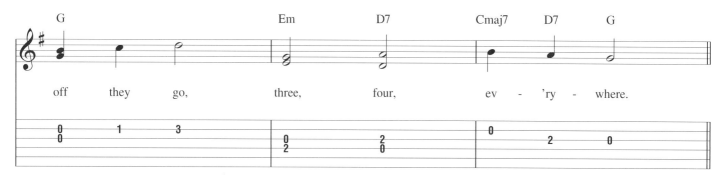

Verse

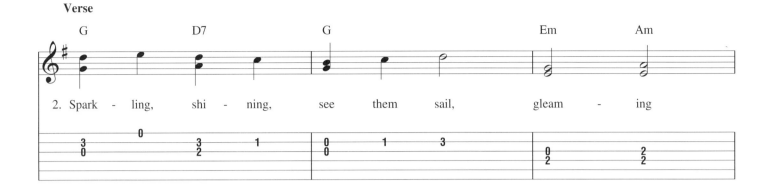

2. Spark - ling, shi - ning, see them sail, gleam - ing

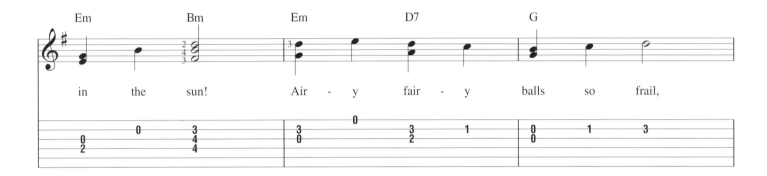

in the sun! Air - y fair - y balls so frail,

Outro

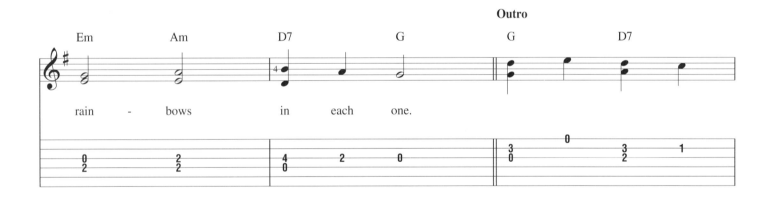

rain - bows in each one.

Rain - bows in each one.

Bobby Shaftoe

Traditional English

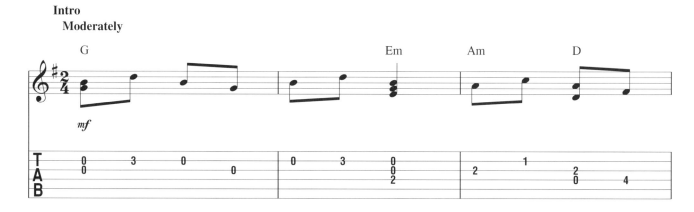

Strum Pattern: 10
Pick Pattern: 10

Intro
Moderately

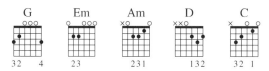

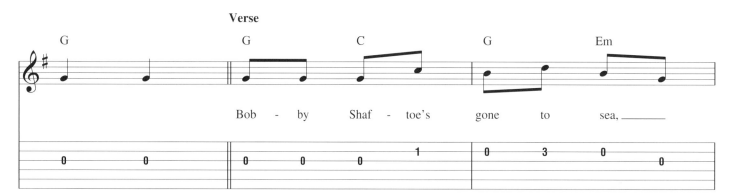

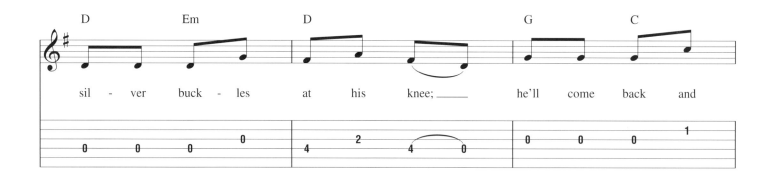

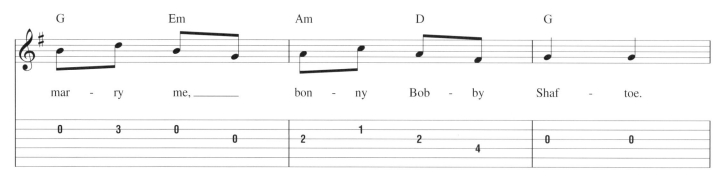

Bob - by Shaf - toe's bright and fair, comb - ing down his

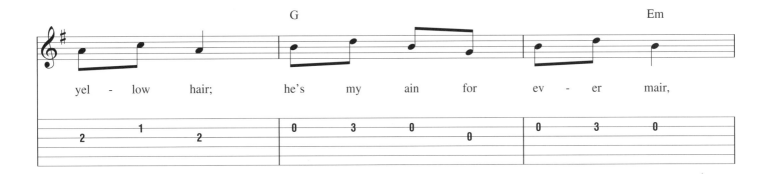

yel - low hair; he's my ain for ev - er mair,

Outro

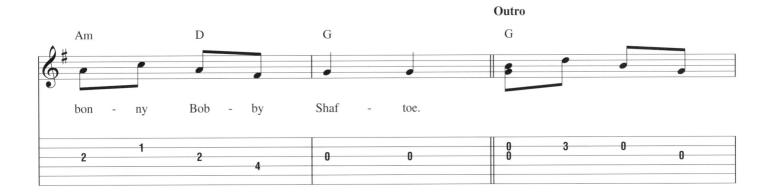

bon - ny Bob - by Shaf - toe.

Camptown Races

Words and Music by Stephen C. Foster

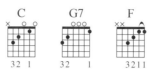

Strum Pattern: 3
Pick Pattern: 4

1. Camp-town la - dies sing this song, doo - dah, _____ doo - dah. _____
2. - 4. *See additional lyrics*

Camp - town race - track five miles long, oh, _____ doo - dah day. _____

Come down there with my hat caved in, doo - dah, _____ doo - dah, _____

Chorus

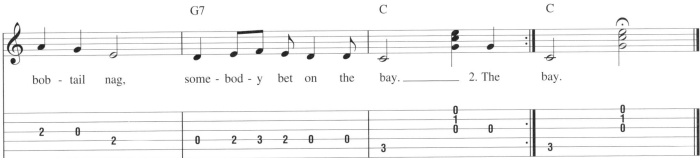

Additional Lyrics

2. The long-tail filly and the big black hoss, doo-dah, doo-dah.
   They fly the track and they both cut across, oh, doo-dah day.
   The blind hoss sticken in a big mud hole, doo-dah, doo-dah.
   Can't touch bottom with a ten-foot pole, oh, doo-dah day.

3. Old muley cow come onto the track, etc.
   The bobtail fling her over his back,
   Then fly along like a railroad car,
   Running a race with a shooting star,

4. See them flying on a ten-mile heat, etc.
   'Round the race track, then repeat,
   I win my money on the bobtail nag,
   I keep my money in an old towbag,

Chook Chook

Traditional

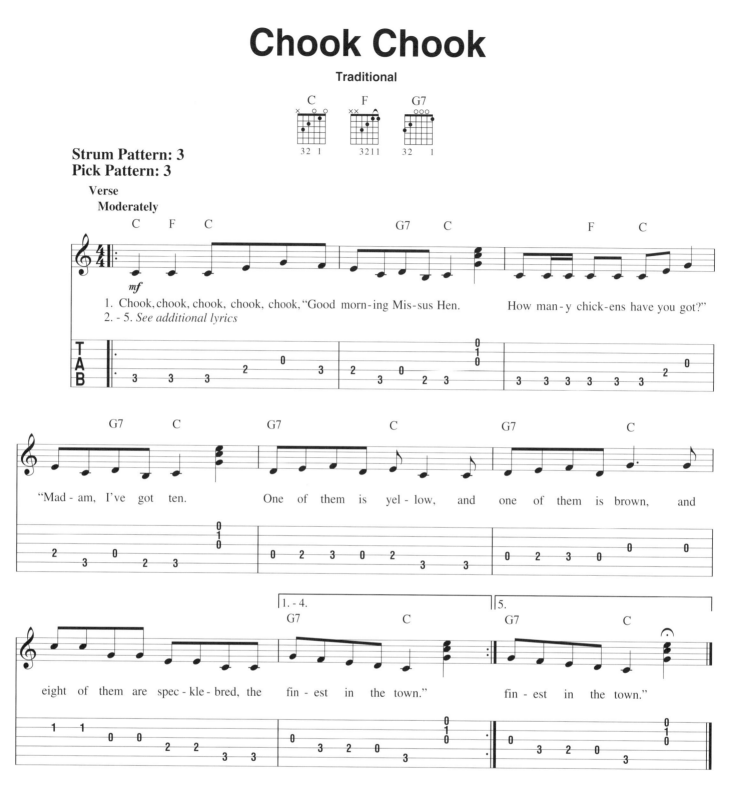

Strum Pattern: 3
Pick Pattern: 3

Verse
Moderately

1. Chook, chook, chook, chook, chook, "Good morn-ing Mis-sus Hen. How man-y chick-ens have you got?"
2. - 5. *See additional lyrics*

"Mad - am, I've got ten. One of them is yel - low, and one of them is brown, and

eight of them are spec - kle - bred, the fin - est in the town." fin - est in the town."

Additional Lyrics

2. Chook, chook, chook, chook, chook,
"Good morning Missus Hen.
How many chickens have you got?"
"Madam, I've got ten.
Two of them are yellow,
And two of them are brown,
And six of them are speckle-bred,
The finest in the town."

3. Chook, chook, chook, chook, chook,
"Good morning Missus Hen.
How many chickens have you got?"
"Madam, I've got ten.
Three of them are yellow,
And three of them are brown,
And four of them are speckle-bred,
The finest in the town."

4. Chook, chook, chook, chook, chook,
"Good morning Missus Hen.
How many chickens have you got?"
"Madam, I've got ten.
Four of them are yellow,
And four of them are brown,
And two of them are speckle-bred,
The finest in the town."

5. Chook, chook, chook, chook, chook,
"Good morning Missus Hen.
How many chickens have you got?"
"Madam, I've got ten.
Five of them are yellow,
And five of them are brown,
And none of them are speckle-bred,
The finest in the town."

Cock-a-Doodle-Doo

Traditional

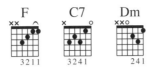

Strum Pattern: 7
Pick Pattern: 7

Additional Lyrics

2. Cock-a-doodle doo!
   What is my dame to do?
   Till master finds his fiddling stick,
   She'll dance without her shoe.
   She'll dance without her shoe,
   She'll dance without her shoe,
   Till master finds his fiddling stick,
   She'll dance without her shoe.

Curly Locks

Traditional

Strum Pattern: 8
Pick Pattern: 8

Cur - ly Locks, Cur - ly Locks, when thou be mine, thou

shalt not wash dish - es nor yet feed the swine, but

sit on a cush - ion and sew a fine seam, and

feed up on straw - ber - ries, sug - ar and cream.

Diddle, Diddle Dumpling, My Son John

Traditional

Daddy Fox

Traditional

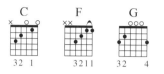

Strum Pattern: 3
Pick Pattern: 3

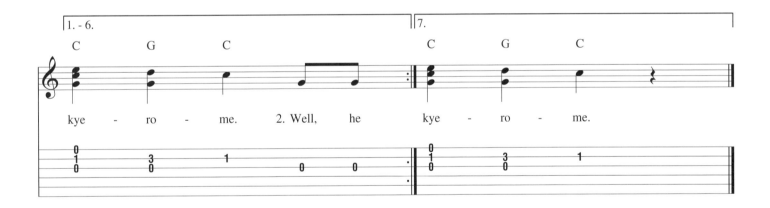

Additional Lyrics

2. Well, he ran 'til he came to a great big pen,
   With a ling-tong dilly-dong kye-ro-me;
   And the ducks and the geese were kept therein,
   With a ling-tong dilly-dong kye-ro-me.

3. He grabbed the grey goose by the neck,
   With a ling-tong dilly-dong kye-ro-me;
   And up with the little ones over his back,
   With a ling-tong dilly-dong kye-ro-me.

4. Old Mother Flipper-Flopper jumped out of bed,
   With a ling-tong dilly-dong kye-ro-me;
   Out of the window she stuck her little head,
   With a ling-tong dilly-dong kye-ro-me.

5. John, he ran to the top of the hill,
   With a ling-tong dilly-dong kye-ro-me;
   And he blew his little horn both loud and shrill,
   With a ling-tong dilly-dong kye-ro-me.

6. The fox, he ran to his cozy den,
   With a ling-tong dilly-dong kye-ro-me;
   And there were the little ones, eight, nine, ten,
   With a ling-tong dilly-dong kye-ro-me.

7. Then the fox and his wife, without any strife,
   With a ling-tong dilly-dong kye-ro-me;
   They cut up the goose with a carving knife,
   With a ling-tong dilly-dong kye-ro-me.

Ding Dong Bell

Traditional

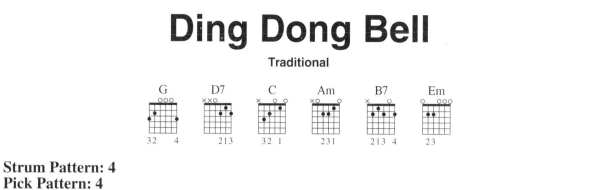

Strum Pattern: 4
Pick Pattern: 4

Verse
Moderately

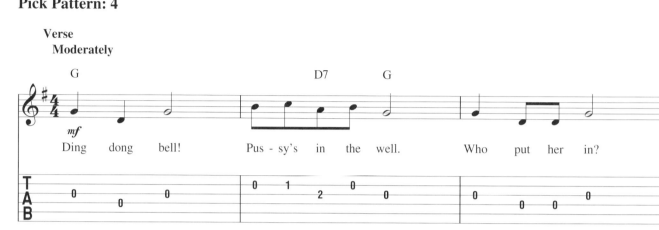

Ding dong bell! Pus - sy's in the well. Who put her in?

Lit - tle Tom - my Green. Who pulled her out? Lit - tle Tom - my Stout. What a

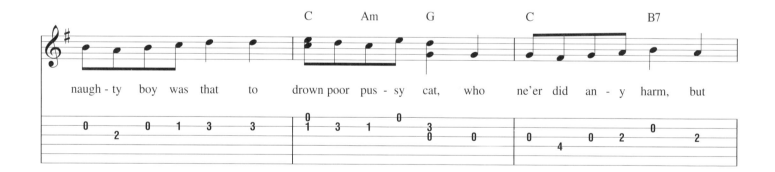

naugh - ty boy was that to drown poor pus - sy cat, who ne'er did an - y harm, but

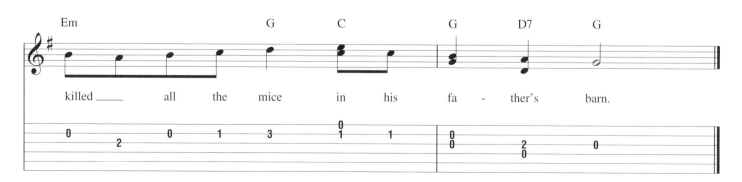

killed _____ all the mice in his fa - ther's barn.

Do Your Ears Hang Low?

Traditional

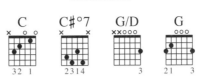

Strum Pattern: 3, 2
Pick Pattern: 4

Intro
Moderately

Doctor Foster

Traditional

Dry Bones

Traditional

Strum Pattern: 3
Pick Pattern: 3

Chorus
Rhythmically

E - ze - kiel cried, "Them dry bones!" E - ze - kiel cried, "Them dry bones!" E -

ze - kiel cried, "Them dry bones!" Oh, hear the word of the Lord! _____ 1. The

Verse

foot bone con - nect - ed to the leg bone, the leg bone con - nect - ed to the

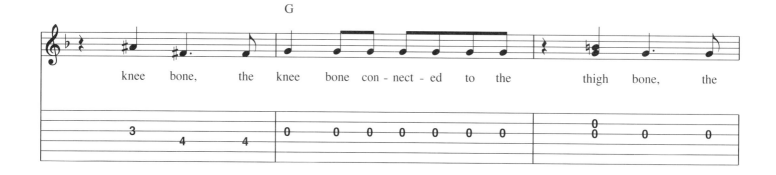

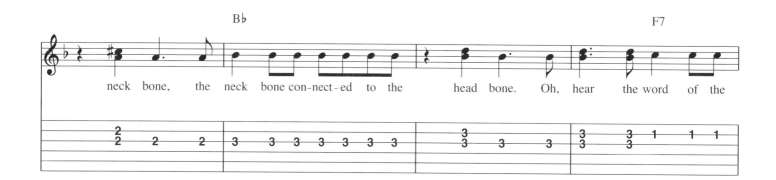

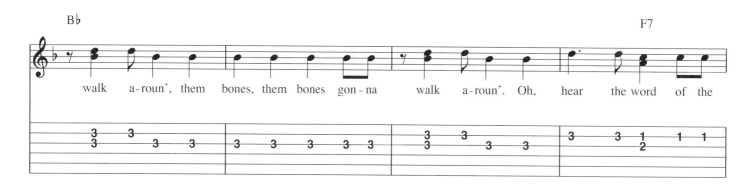

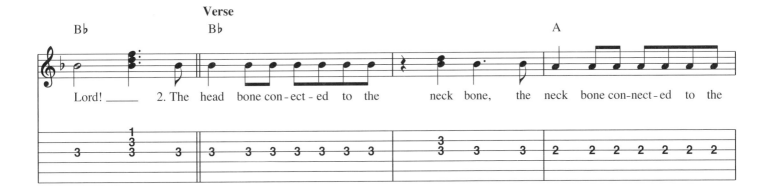

Verse

Lord! _____ 2. The head bone con-ect-ed to the neck bone, the neck bone con-nect-ed to the

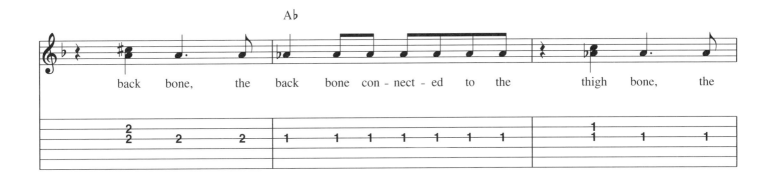

back bone, the back bone con-nect-ed to the thigh bone, the

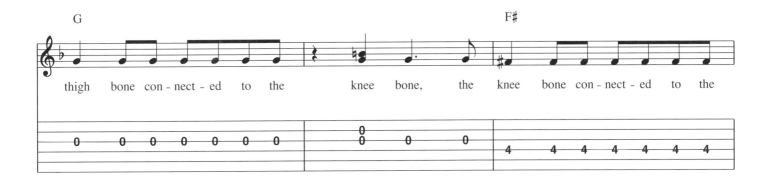

thigh bone con-nect-ed to the knee bone, the knee bone con-nect-ed to the

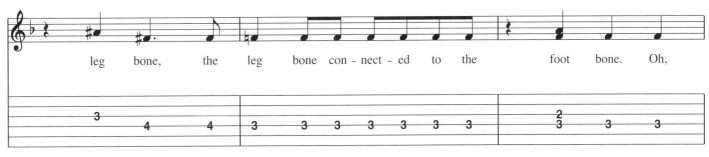

leg bone, the leg bone con-nect-ed to the foot bone. Oh,

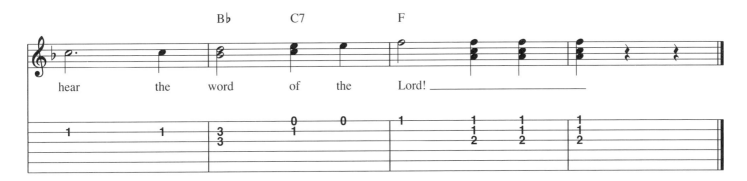

hear the word of the Lord! _____

The Drunken Sailor

American Sea Chantey

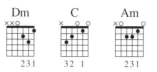

Strum Pattern: 3
Pick Pattern: 5

1. What shall we do with the drunk - en sail - or?
2. - 5. *See additional lyrics*

What shall we do with the drunk - en sail - or? What shall we do with the

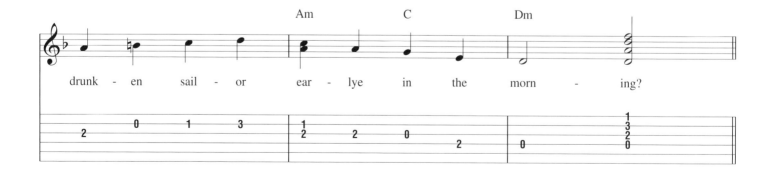

drunk - en sail - or ear - lye in the morn - ing?

Chorus

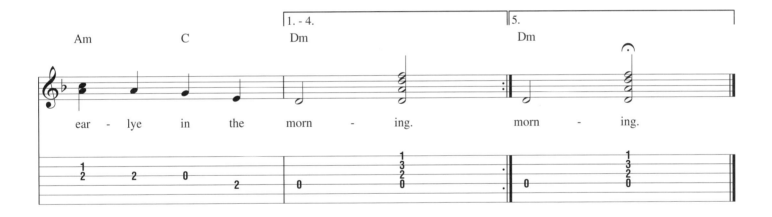

Additional Lyrics

2. Put him in the long boat till he's sober,
   Put him in the long boat till he's sober,
   Put him in the long boat till he's sober
   Earlye in the morning

3. Pull out the plug and wet him all over,
   Pull out the plug and wet him all over,
   Pull out the plug and wet him all over
   Earlye in the morning.

4. Tie him to the top mast when she's under,
   Tie him to the top mast when she's under,
   Tie him to the top mast when she's under
   Earlye in the morning.

5. Put him in the scruppers with the hosepipe on him,
   Put him in the scruppers with the hosepipe on him,
   Put him in the scruppers with the hosepipe on him
   Earlye in the morning.

Eensy Weensy Spider

Traditional

C   G7   Am   D7

Strum Pattern: 8
Pick Pattern: 8

Moderately, in 2

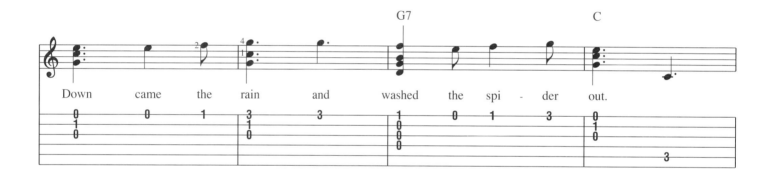

The een - sy ween - sy spi - der went up the wa - ter spout.

Down came the rain and washed the spi - der out.

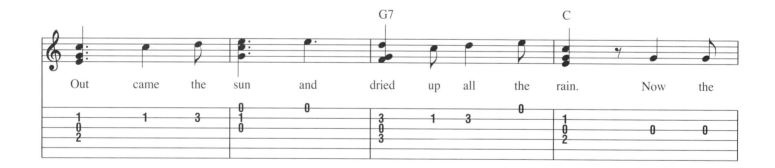

Out came the sun and dried up all the rain. Now the

een - sy ween - sy spi - der went up the spout a - gain.

The Farmer in the Dell

Traditional

Strum Pattern: 8
Pick Pattern: 8

Additional Lyrics

2. The farmer takes a wife,
The farmer takes a wife,
Heigh ho, the derry oh,
The farmer takes a wife.

3. The wife takes a child, etc.

4. The child takes a nurse, etc.

5. The nurse takes a dog, etc.

6. The dog takes a cat, etc.

7. The cat takes a rat, etc.

8. The rat takes the cheese, etc.

9. The cheese stands alone, etc.

Fee! Fi! Foe! Fum!

Traditional

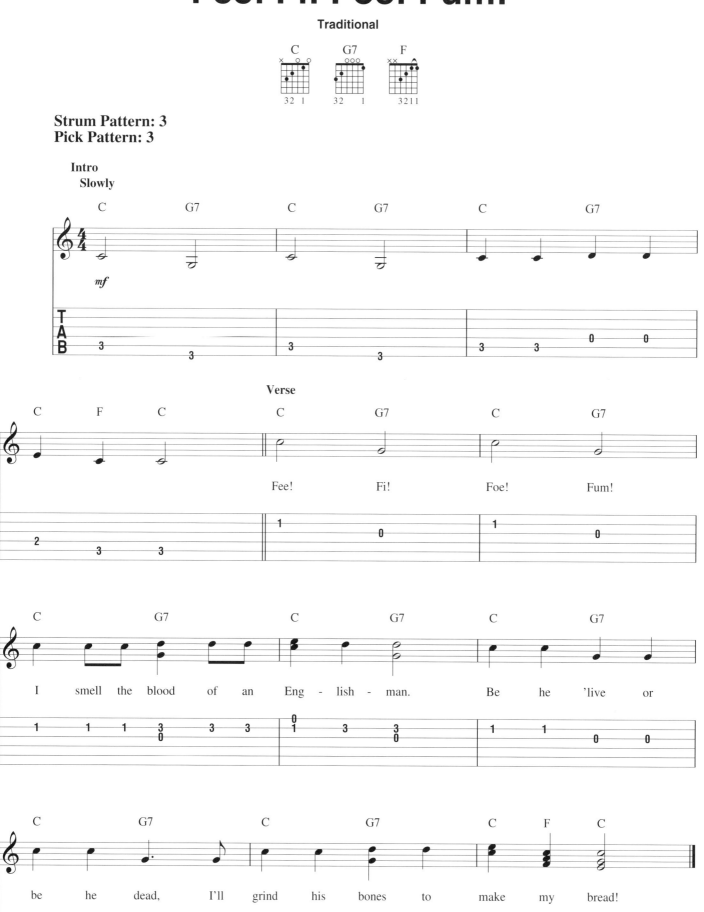

Strum Pattern: 3
Pick Pattern: 3

Fiddle-De-Dee

Traditional

Strum Pattern: 8
Pick Pattern: 8

Additional Lyrics

2. Fiddle-de-dee, fiddle-de-dee,
   The fly has married the bumblebee.
   Says the bee, says she, "I'll live under your wing,
   And you'll never know I carry a sting."
   Fiddle-de-dee. fiddle-de-dee,
   The fly has married the bumblebee.

3. Fiddle-de-dee, fiddle-de-dee,
   The fly has married the bumblebee.
   And when parson Beetle had married the pair,
   They both went out to take the air.
   Fiddle-de-dee. fiddle-de-dee,
   The fly has married the bumblebee.

Five Little Ducks

Traditional

Strum Pattern: 4
Pick Pattern: 4

Additional Lyrics

2. Four little ducks went swimming one day,
   Over the hills and far away.
   The mother duck said, "Quack, quack, quack, quack,"
   And only three little ducks came back.

3. Three little ducks went swimming one day,
   Over the hills and far away.
   The mother duck said, "Quack, quack, quack, quack,"
   And only two little ducks came back.

4. Two little ducks went swimming one day,
   Over the hills and far away.
   The mother duck said, "Quack, quack, quack, quack,"
   And only one little duck came back.

5. One little duck went swimming one day,
   Over the hills and far away.
   The mother duck said, "Quack, quack, quack, quack,"
   And five little ducks came swimming right back.

Found a Peanut

Traditional

C   G   Dm

Strum Pattern: 9
Pick Pattern: 9

Verse

Moderately

C

1. Found a pea - nut, found a pea - nut, found a pea - nut last ___ night.

2. - 12. *See additional lyrics*

G   Dm   G   C

night. Last ___ night I found a pea - nut, found a

G

1. - 11.   C

pea - nut last ___ night. 2. Where'd you

12.   C

night.

Additional Lyrics

2. Where'd you find it? Where'd you find it?
   Where'd you find it last night?
   Last night, where'd you find it?
   Where'd you find it last night?

3. In a dustbin, in a dustbin,
   In a dustbin last night.
   Last night, in a dustbin,
   In a dustbin last night.

4. Cracked it open, cracked it open,
   Cracked it open last night.
   Last night I cracked it open,
   Cracked it open last night.

5. Found it rotten, found it rotten,
   Found it rotten last night.
   Last night I found it rotten,
   Found it rotten last night.

6. Ate it anyway, ate it anyway,
   Ate it anyway last night.
   Last night I ate it anyway,
   Ate it anyway last night.

7. I felt sick, I felt sick,
   I felt sick last night.
   Last night I felt sick,
   I felt sick last night.

8. Called the doctor, called the doctor,
   Called the doctor last night.
   Last night I called the doctor,
   Called the doctor last night.

9. Went to heaven, went to heaven,
   Went to heaven last night.
   Last night I went to heaven,
   Went to heaven last night.

10. Didn't want me, didn't want me,
    Didn't want me last night.
    Last night they didn't want me,
    Didn't want me last night.

11. Went the other way, went the other way,
    Went the other way last night.
    Last night I went the other way,
    Went the other way last night.

12. Shovelling coal, shovelling coal,
    Shovelling coal last night.
    Last night I was shovelling coal,
    Shovelling coal last night.

Five Little Speckled Frogs

Traditional

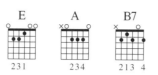

Strum Pattern: 10
Pick Pattern: 10

to the pool, where it _____ was nice and cool,

now there _____ are just four speck - led frogs. Glub!

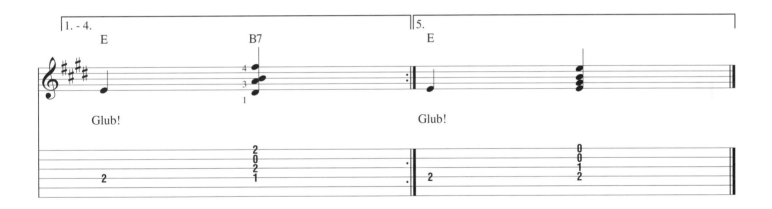

Glub! Glub!

Additional Lyrics

2. Four little speckled frogs
Sat on a speckled log,
Eating some most delicious bugs.
Yum! Yum!
One jumped into the pool,
Where it was nice and cool,
Now there are just three speckled frogs.
Glub! Glub!

3. Three little speckled frogs
Sat on a speckled log,
Eating some most delicious bugs.
Yum! Yum!
One jumped into the pool,
Where it was nice and cool,
Now there are just two speckled frogs.
Glub! Glub!

4. Two little speckled frogs
Sat on a speckled log,
Eating some most delicious bugs.
Yum! Yum!
One jumped into the pool,
Where it was nice and cool,
Now there is just one speckled frog.
Glub! Glub!

5. One little speckled frog
Sat on a speckled log,
Eating some most delicious bugs.
Yum! Yum!
One jumped into the pool,
Where it was nice and cool,
Now there are no more speckled frogs.
Glub! Glub!

Frère Jacques

(Are You Sleeping?)

Traditional

Strum Pattern: 5
Pick Pattern: 1

Frog Went A-Courtin'

Traditional

Strum Pattern: 4
Pick Pattern: 5

Verse

Happily

1. Oh, frog went a-court-in' and he did ride, uh-huh, _____ uh-
2. – 15. *See additional lyrics*

huh. Frog went a-court-in' and he did ride, ___ sword and pis-tol

by his side, uh-huh, _____ uh-huh. 2. Well, huh.

Additional Lyrics

2. Well, he rode down to Miss Mousie's door, uh-huh, uh-huh,
   Well, he rode down to Miss Mousie's door,
   Where he had often been before, uh-huh, uh-huh.

3. He took Miss Mousie on his knee, uh-huh, uh-huh,
   He took Miss Mousie on his knee,
   Said, "Miss Mousie will you marry me?" Uh-huh, uh-huh.

4. "I'll have to ask my Uncle Rat, etc.
   See what he will say to that." etc.

5. "Without my Uncle Rat's consent,
   I would not marry the President."

6. Well, Uncle Rat laughed
   And shook his fat sides,
   To think his niece would be a bride.

7. Well, Uncle Rat rode off to town,
   To buy his niece a wedding gown.

8. "Where will the wedding supper be?"
   "Way down yonder in a hollow tree."

9. "What will the wedding supper be?"
   "A fried mosquito and a roasted flea."

10. First to come in were two little ants,
    Fixing around to have a dance.

11. Next to come in was a bumble bee,
    Bouncing a fiddle on his knee.

12. Next to come in was a fat sassy lad,
    Thinks himself as big as his dad.

13. Thinks himself a man indeed,
    Because he chews the tobacco weed.

14. And next to come in was a big tomcat,
    He swallowed the frog
    And the mouse and the rat.

15. Next to come in was a big old snake,
    He chased the party into the lake.

Georgie Porgie

Traditional

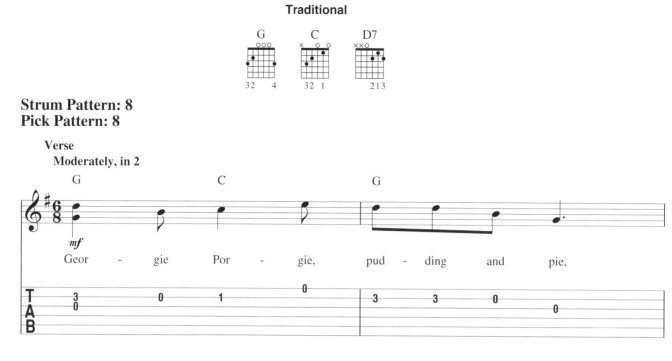

Strum Pattern: 8
Pick Pattern: 8

Verse
Moderately, in 2

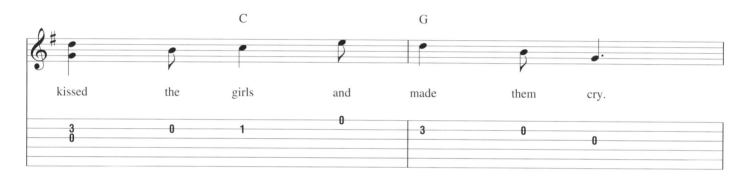

Geor - gie Por - gie, pud - ding and pie,

kissed the girls and made them cry.

When the boys came out to play,

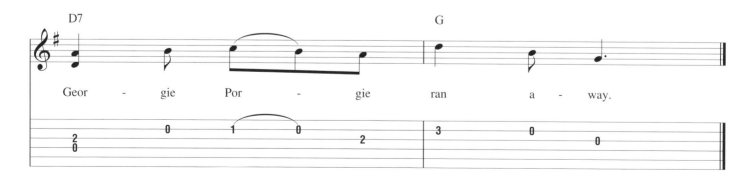

Geor - gie Por - gie ran a - way.

Goosey, Goosey Gander

Traditional

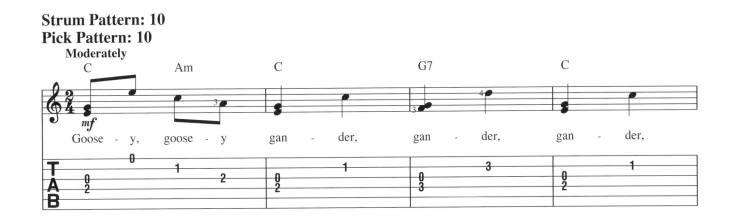

Strum Pattern: 10
Pick Pattern: 10

Moderately

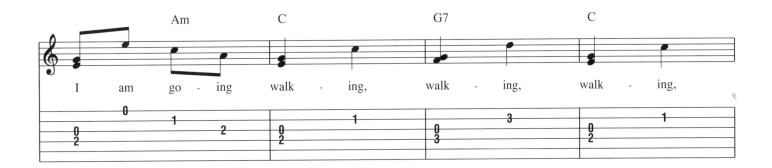

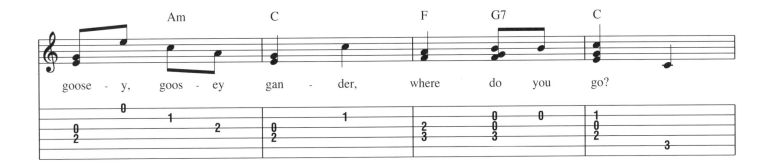

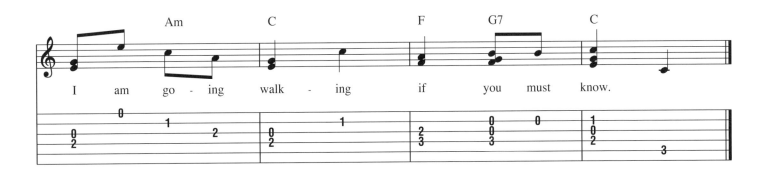

Ging Gang Gooli

Traditional

Strum Pattern: 3
Pick Pattern: 3

Verse

Moderately fast

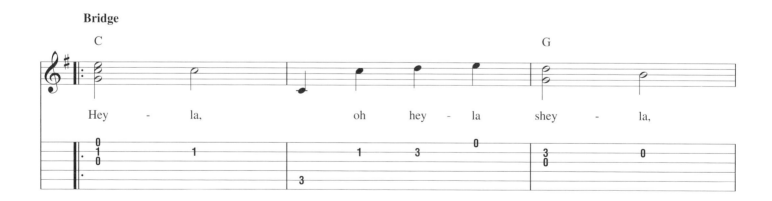

Ging gang goo - li goo - li goo - li goo - li wat - cha ging gang

goo, ging gang goo. Ging gang goo!

Bridge

Hey - la, oh hey - la shey - la,

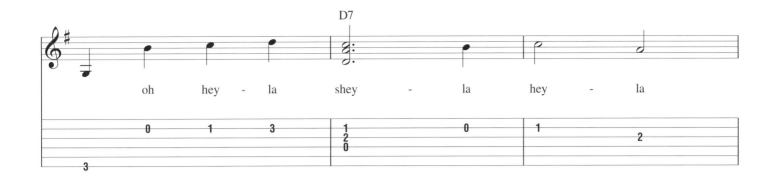

oh hey - la shey - la hey - la

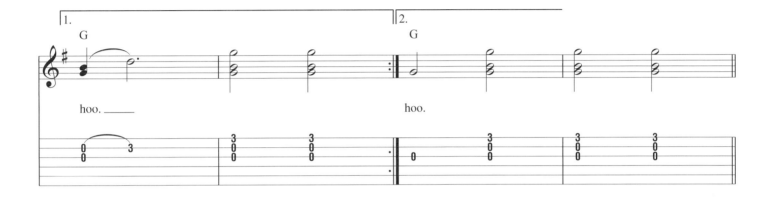

hoo. _____ hoo.

Outro

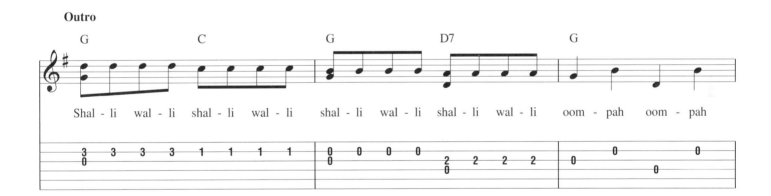

Shal - li wal - li shal - li wal - li shal - li wal - li shal - li wal - li oom - pah oom - pah

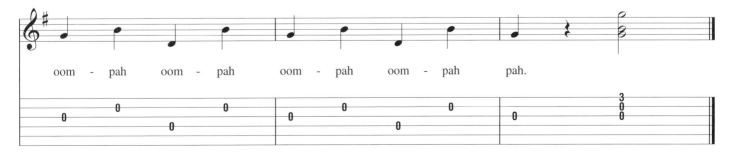

oom - pah oom - pah oom - pah oom - pah pah.

Going Over the Sea

Traditional

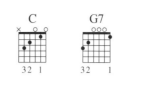

Strum Pattern: 8
Pick Pattern: 8

Verse
Moderately, in 2

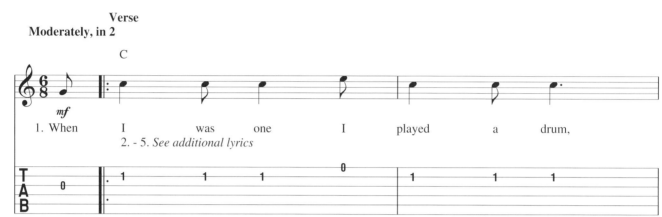

1. When I was one I played a drum,
2. - 5. *See additional lyrics*

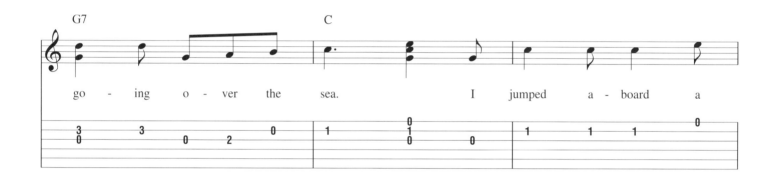

go - ing o - ver the sea. I jumped a - board a

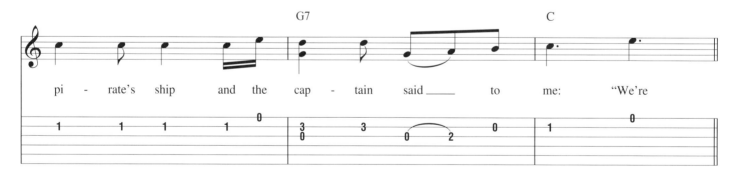

pi - rate's ship and the cap - tain said _____ to me: "We're

Chorus

go - ing this way, that way, for - wards and back - wards,

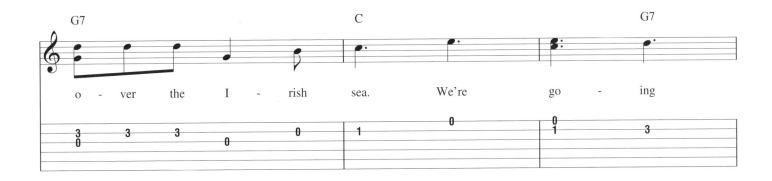

o - ver the I - rish sea. We're go - ing

this way, that way, for - wards and back - wards, o - ver the I - rish

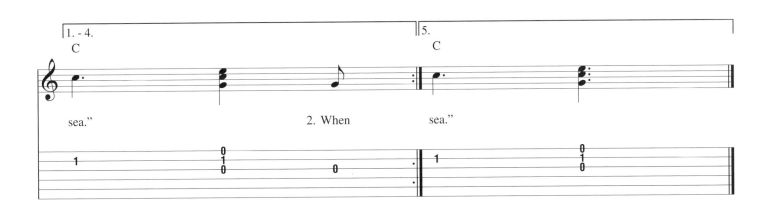

sea." 2. When sea."

Additional Lyrics

2. When I was two I played a kazoo,
   Going over the sea.
   I jumped aboard a pirate's ship
   And the captain said to me:

3. When I was three I sang merrily,
   Going over the sea.
   I jumped aboard a pirate's ship
   And the captain said to me:

4. When I was four I danced on the floor,
   Going over the sea.
   I jumped aboard a pirate's ship
   And the captain said to me:

5. When I was five I did a jive,
   Going over the sea.
   I jumped aboard a pirate's ship
   And the captain said to me:

The Grand Old Duke of York

Traditional Folk Song

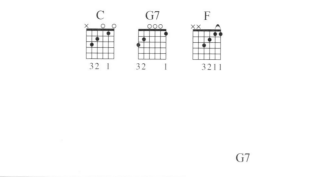

Strum Pattern: 10
Pick Pattern: 10

Verse
Moderately

Oh, the grand old Duke of York, ___ he had ten thou - sand men. ___ He

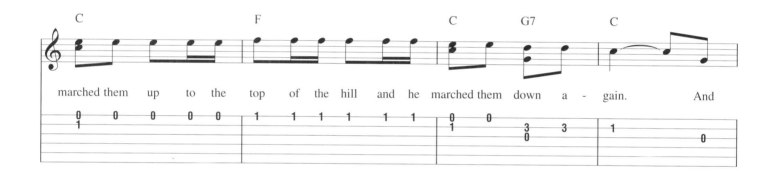

marched them up to the top of the hill and he marched them down a - gain. And

when they were up, they were up, ___ and when they were down, they were down. ___ And

when they were on - ly half way up, they were nei - ther up nor down.

Hark, Hark, the Dogs Do Bark

Traditional

Strum Pattern: 8
Pick Pattern: 8

Grandfather's Clock

By Henry Clay Work

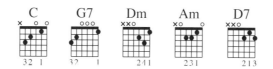

Strum Pattern: 3
Pick Pattern: 3

Verse
Moderately slow

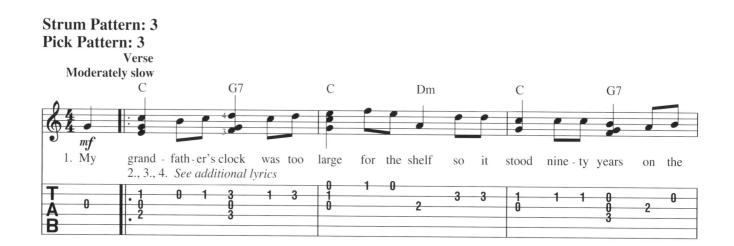

1. My grand-fath-er's clock was too large for the shelf so it stood nine-ty years on the
2., 3., 4. *See additional lyrics*

floor. ___ It was tall-er by half than the old man him-self though it weighed not a pen-ny-weight

more. ___ It was bought on the morn of the day that he was born and was al-ways his trea-sure and

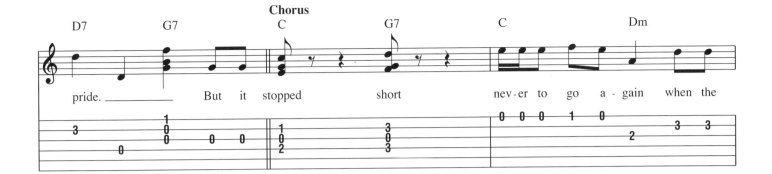

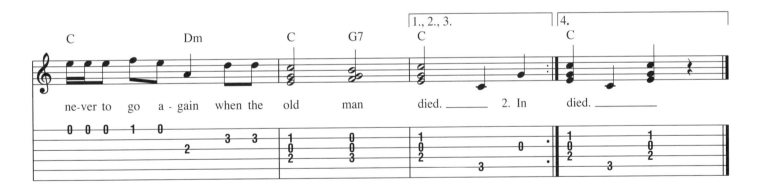

Additional Lyrics

2. In watching its pendulum swing to and fro,
Many hours had he spent while a boy;
And in childhood and manhood the clock seemed to know,
And to share both his grief and his joy.
For it struck twenty-four when he entered at the door,
With a blooming and beautiful bride.

3. My grandfather said that of those he could hire,
Not a servant so faithful he found;
For it wasted no time, and had but one desire,
At the close of each week to be wound.
And it kept in its place, not a frown upon its face,
And its hands never hung by its side.

4. It rang an alarm in the dead of the night,
An alarm that for years had been dumb;
And we knew that his spirit was pluming its flight,
That his hour of departure had come.
Still the clock kept the time, with a soft and muffled chime,
As we silently stood by his side.

Green Grow the Rushes, O

Traditional Irish Folk Song

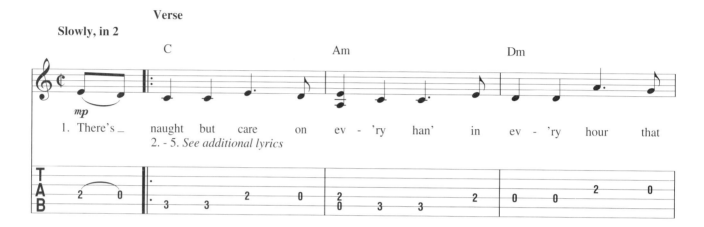

Strum Pattern: 3
Pick Pattern: 2

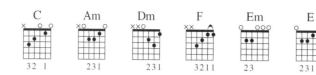

Slowly, in 2

1. There's __ naught but care on ev - 'ry han' in ev - 'ry hour that
2. - 5. *See additional lyrics*

pass - es, O; what sig - ni - fies that life o' man, an'

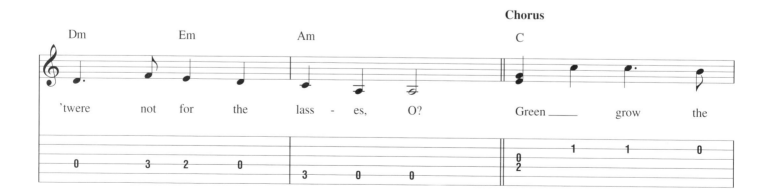

'twere not for the lass - es, O? Green ____ grow the

rush - es, O.   Green ___ grow the rush - es, O;   the

sweet - est hours that ___ e'er   I spend are spent a - mong the

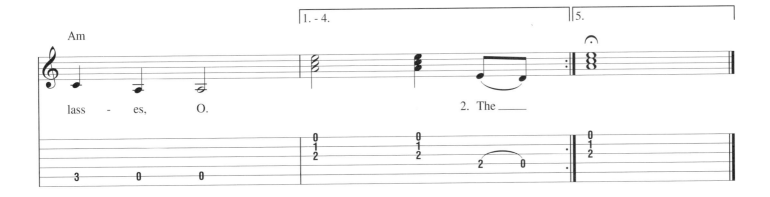

lass - es, O.   2. The ___

Additional Lyrics

2. The worldly race may riches chase,
   An' riches still may fly them, O;
   An' though at last they catch them fast,
   Their hearts can ne'er enjoy them, O.

3. Gie me a cannie hour at e'en,
   My arms around my dearie, O;
   An' worldly cares an' worldly men
   May a' gae tapsalteerie, O!

4. An' you sae douce, ye sneer at this,
   Ye're naught but senseless asses, O;
   The wisest man the world e'er saw,
   He dearly loved the lasses, O.

5. Auld nature swears the lovely dears,
   Her noblest work she classes, O;
   Her prentice han' she tried on man,
   An' then she made the lasses, O.

Have a Little Dog

Traditional

Strum Pattern: 3
Pick Pattern: 3

Verse
Moderately

1. Have a lit - tle dog and his name is Don,
2. - 8. *See additional lyrics*

have a lit - tle dog and his name is Don, his legs go to feet and his

bod - y goes to tongue, toll - a - wink - er, toll - a - wink - er, tum toll - y - aye. toll - y - aye.

Additional Lyrics

2. Have a little box about three feet square,
   Have a little box about three feet square,
   When I go to travel I put him in there,
   Toll-a-winker, toll-a-winker, tum-tolly-aye.

3. When I go to travel, I travel like an ox,
   When I go to travel, I travel like an ox,
   And in that vest pocket I carry that box,
   Toll-a-winker, toll-a-winker, tum-tolly-aye.

4. Had a little hen and her colour was fair,
   Had a little hen and her colour was fair,
   Sat her on a bomb and she hatched me a hare,
   Toll-a-winker, toll-a-winker, tum-tolly-aye.

5. The hare turned a horse about six fee high,
   The hare turned a horse about six fee high,
   If you want to beat this, you'll have to tell a lie,
   Toll-a-winker, toll-a-winker, tum-tolly-aye.

6. I had a little mule and his name was Jack,
   I had a little mule and his name was Jack,
   I rode him on his tail to save his back,
   Toll-a-winker, toll-a-winker, tum-tolly-aye.

7. I had a little mule and his name was Jay,
   I had a little mule and his name was Jay,
   I pulled his tail to hear him bray,
   Toll-a-winker, toll-a-winker, tum-tolly-aye.

8. I had a little mule, he was made of hay,
   I had a little mule, he was made of hay,
   First big wind come along and blew him away,
   Toll-a-winker, toll-a-winker, tum-tolly-aye.

Head, Shoulders, Knees and Toes

Traditional

Strum Pattern: 3
Pick Pattern: 3

Additional Lyrics

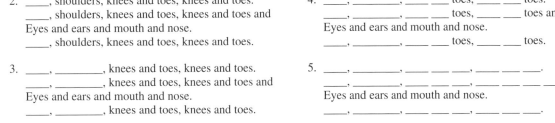

2. ____, shoulders, knees and toes, knees and toes.
    ____, shoulders, knees and toes, knees and toes and
    Eyes and ears and mouth and nose.
    ____, shoulders, knees and toes, knees and toes.

3. Head, _____, knees and toes, knees and toes.
    ____, _____, knees and toes, knees and toes and
    Eyes and ears and mouth and nose.
    ____, _____, _____, knees and toes, knees and toes.

4. ____, _____, ____ ____ toes, ____ ____ toes.
    ____, _____, ____ ____ toes, ____ ____ toes and
    Eyes and ears and mouth and nose.
    ____, _____, _____, ____ ____ toes, ____ ____ toes.

5. ____, _____, ____ ____ ____, ____ ____ ____.
    ____, _____, ____ ____ ____, ____ ____ ____ and
    Eyes and ears and mouth and nose.
    ____, _____, _____, ____ ____ ____, ____ ____ ____.

Here We Go Gathering Nuts in May

Traditional

Strum Pattern: 7
Pick Pattern: 7

Additional Lyrics

2. Who will you have for nuts in May,
   Nuts in May, nuts in May?
   Who will you have for nuts in May,
   All on a summer's morning?

3. We'll have ____ for nuts in May,
   Nuts in May, nuts in May.
   We'll have ____ for nuts in May,
   All on a summer's morning.

4. Who will you send to fetch her/him away,
   Fetch her/him away, fetch her/him away?
   Who will you send to fetch her/him away,
   All on a summer's morning?

5. We'll send ____ to fetch her/him away,
   Fetch her/him away, fetch her/him away?
   We'll send ____ to fetch her/him away,
   All on a summer's morning.

Hey Diddle Diddle

Traditional

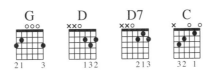

Strum Pattern: 8
Pick Pattern: 8

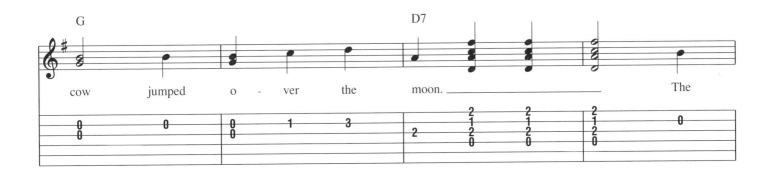

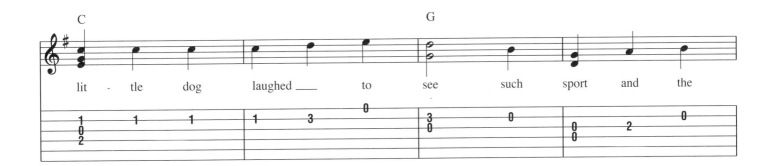

Here We Go Looby Loo

Traditional Folk Song

Strum Pattern: 8
Pick Pattern: 8

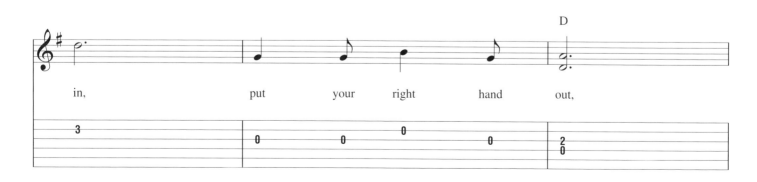

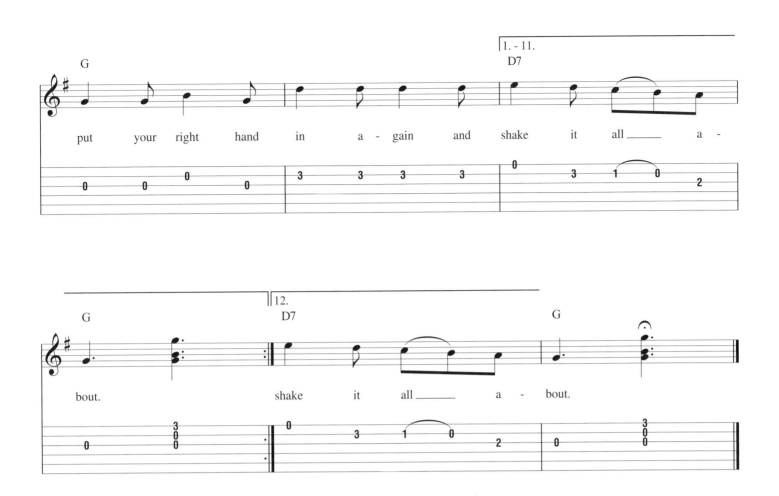

Additional Lyrics

2. Put your left hand in,
   Put your left hand out,
   Put your left hand in again
   And shake it all about.

3. Put your right arm in,
   Put your right arm out,
   Put your right arm in again
   And shake it all about.

4. Put your left arm in,
   Put your left arm out,
   Put your left arm in again
   And shake it all about.

5. Put your right foot in,
   Put your right foot out,
   Put your right foot in again
   And shake it all about.

6. Put your left foot in,
   Put your left foot out,
   Put your left foot in again
   And shake it all about.

7. Put your right leg in,
   Put your right leg out,
   Put your right leg in again
   And shake it all about.

8. Put your left leg in,
   Put your left leg out,
   Put your left leg in again
   And shake it all about.

9. Put your back in,
   Put your back out,
   Put your back in again
   And shake it all about.

10. Put your front in,
    Put your front out,
    Put your front in again
    And shake it all about.

11. Put your head in,
    Put your head out,
    Put your head in again
    And shake it all about.

12. Put your whole self in,
    Put your whole self out,
    Put your whole self in again
    And shake it all about.

Hickory Dickory Dock

Traditional

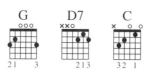

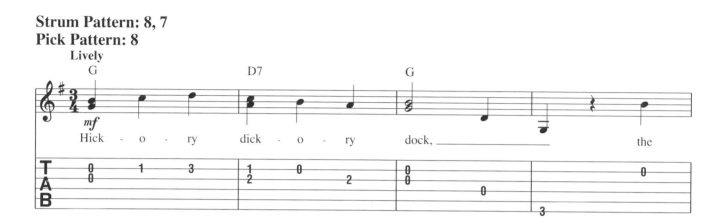

Strum Pattern: 8, 7
Pick Pattern: 8

Lively

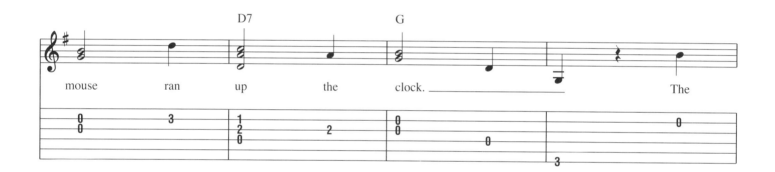

Hick - o - ry dick - o - ry dock, _____ the

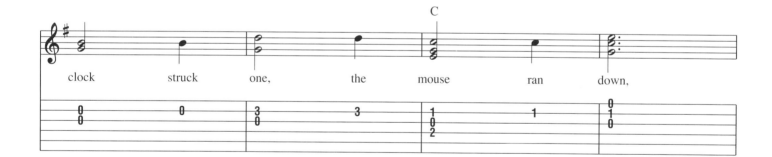

mouse ran up the clock. _____ The

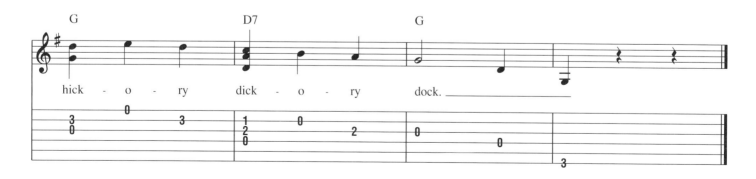

clock struck one, the mouse ran down,

hick - o - ry dick - o - ry dock. _____

Hob Shoe Hob

Traditional

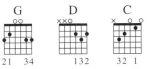

Strum Pattern: 3
Pick Pattern: 3

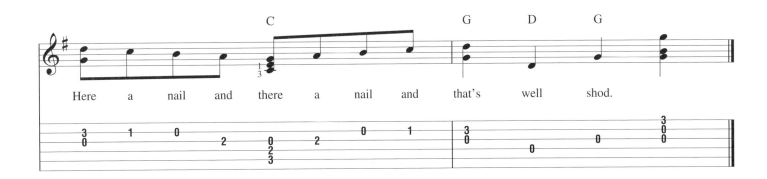

Hot Cross Buns

Traditional

Strum Pattern: 10
Pick Pattern: 10

Moderately

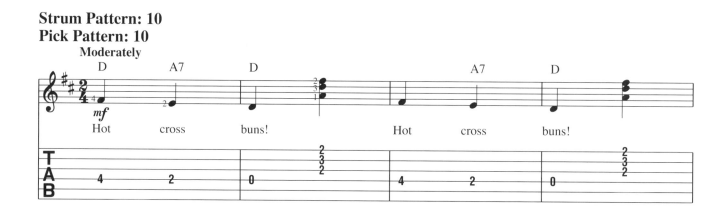

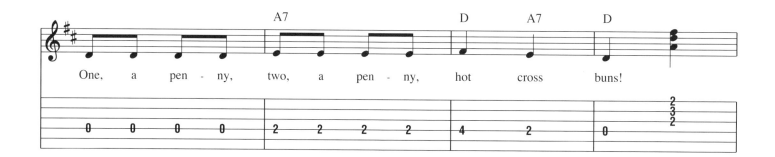

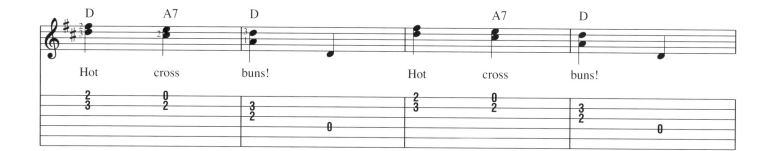

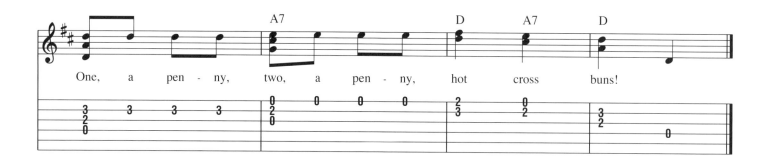

Humpty Dumpty

Traditional

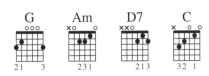

Strum Pattern: 8
Pick Pattern: 8

Brightly

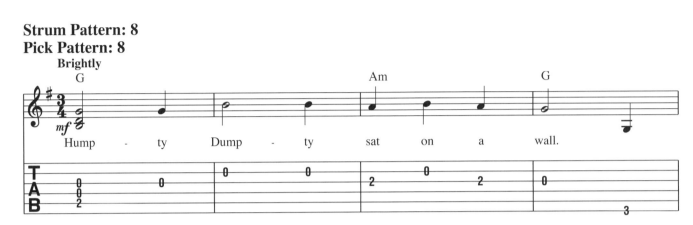

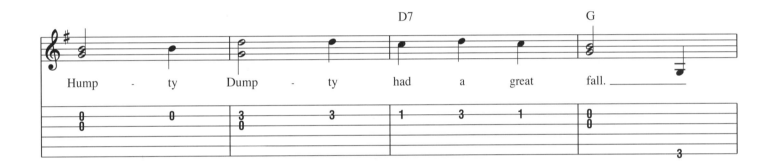

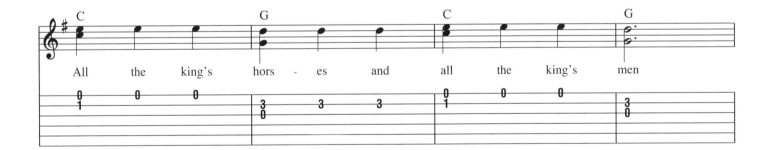

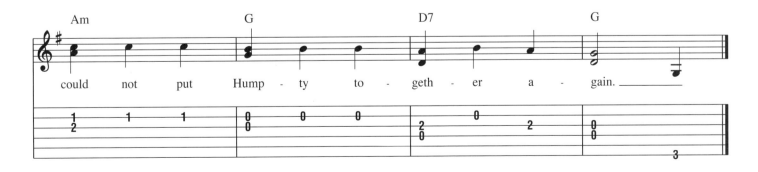

Hush-a-Bye, Baby

Traditional

Strum Pattern: 7
Pick Pattern: 7

Intro
Moderately slow

Verse

Hush - a - bye, ba - by,

on the tree top. When the wind blows, the cra - dle will rock.

When the bough breaks, the cra - dle will fall. Down will come ba - by,

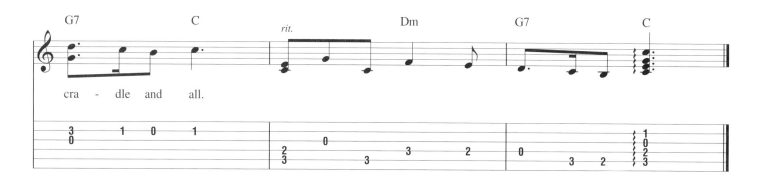

cra - dle and all.

Hush, Little Baby

Carolina Folk Lullaby

Strum Pattern: 3
Pick Pattern: 4

Verse
Moderately

1. Hush, lit-tle ba-by, don't say a word, Pa-pa's gon-na buy you a
2., 3., 4. *See additional lyrics*

mock-ing bird, and if that mock-ing bird won't sing,

1., 2., 3.

Pap-pa's gon-na buy you a dia-mond ring. 2. And ba-by in town. ____

Additional Lyrics

2. And if that diamond ring is brass,
   Papa's gonna buy you a looking glass.
   And if that looking glass gets broke,
   Papa's gonna buy you a billy goat.

3. And if that billy goat don't pull,
   Papa's gonna buy you a cart and bull.
   And if that cart and bull turn over,
   Papa's gonna buy you a dog named Rover.

4. And if that dog named Rover don't bark,
   Papa's gonna buy you a horse and cart.
   And if that horse and cart fall down,
   You'll still be the sweetest little baby in town.

I Had a Little Nut Tree

Traditional

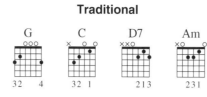

Strum Pattern: 3
Pick Pattern: 3

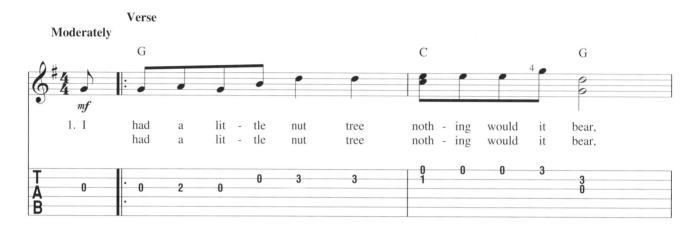

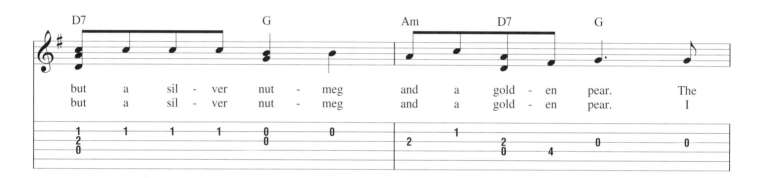

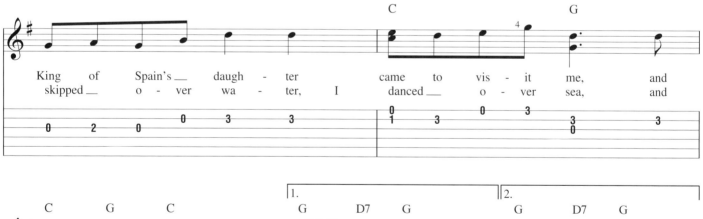

I Know an Old Lady Who Swallowed a Fly

Traditional

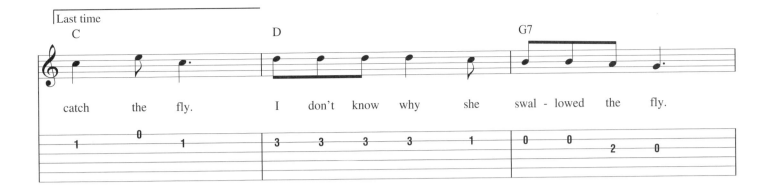

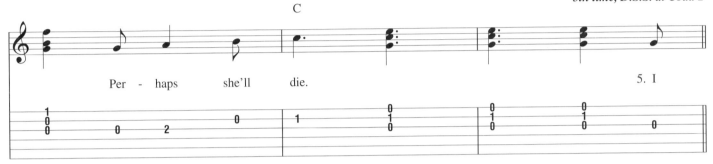

1st-4th times, D.S.S. (take repeats)
5th time, D.S.S. al Coda 2

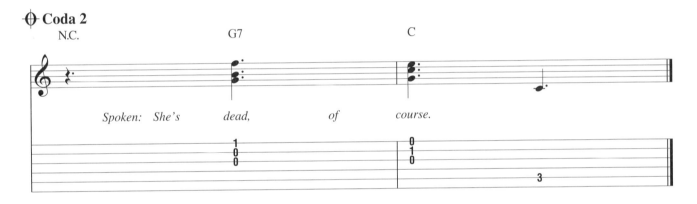

Additional Lyrics

5. I know an old lady who swallowed a dog.
   What a hog, to swallow a dog.
   She swallowed the dog to catch the cat,
   She swallowed the cat to catch the bird,
   She swallowed the bird to catch the spider,
   She swallowed the spider to catch the fly.
   I don't know why she swallowed the fly.
   Perhaps she'll die.

6. I know an old lady who swallowed a goat.
   She just opened her throat and swallowed a goat.
   She swallowed the goat to catch the dog,
   She swallowed the dog to catch the cat,
   She swallowed the cat to catch the bird,
   She swallowed the bird to catch the spider,
   She swallowed the spider to catch the fly.
   I don't know why she swallowed the fly.
   Perhaps she'll die.

7. I know an old lady who swallowed a cow.
   I don't know how she swallowed a cow.
   She swallowed the cow to catch the goat,
   She swallowed the goat to catch the dog,
   She swallowed the dog to catch the cat,
   She swallowed the cat to catch the bird,
   She swallowed the bird to catch the spider,
   She swallowed the spider to catch the fly.
   I don't know why she swallowed the fly.
   Perhaps she'll die.

8. I know an old lady who swallowed a rhinocerous.
   That's proposterous.
   She swallowed the rhino to catch the cow,
   She swallowed the cow to catch the goat,
   She swallowed the goat to catch the dog,
   She swallowed the dog to catch the cat,
   She swallowed the cat to catch the bird,
   She swallowed the bird to catch the spider,
   She swallowed the spider to catch the fly.
   I don't know why she swallowed the fly.
   Perhaps she'll die.

9. I know an old lady who swallowed a horse.
   Spoken: She's dead, of course.

I Love Little Pussy

Traditional

Strum Pattern: 8
Pick Pattern: 8

Verse
Moderately

I ___ love lit - tle pus - sy, her coat is so warm, and

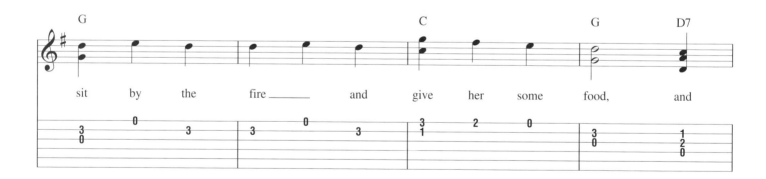

if I don't hurt her, she'll do me no harm. I'll ___

sit by the fire ___ and give her some food, and

pus - sy will love me be - cause I am good.

I'm a Nut

Traditional

Strum Pattern: 3
Pick Pattern: 3

If You're Happy and You Know It

Words and Music by L. Smith

Strum Pattern: 1, 4
Pick Pattern: 2, 5

Verse

Moderately fast

1. If you're hap-py and you know it, clap your hands. (clap, clap) If you're
2., 3. *See additional lyrics*

hap-py and you know it, clap your hands. (clap, clap) If you're hap-py and you know it, then your

face will sure-ly show it, if you're hap-py and you know it clap your hands. (clap, clap) 2. If you're men." ("A-men.")

Additional Lyrics

2. If you're happy and you know it, stomp your feet. (stomp, stomp)
   If you're happy and you know it, stomp your feet. (stomp, stomp)
   If you're happy and you know it, then your face will surely show it.
   If you're happy and you know it, stomp your feet. (stomp, stomp)

3. If you're happy and you know it, say "Amen." ("Amen.")
   If you're happy and you know it, say "Amen." ("Amen.")
   If you're happy and you know it, then your face will surely show it.
   If you're happy and you know it, say "Amen." ("Amen.")

It's Raining, It's Pouring

Traditional

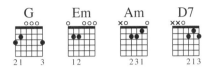

Strum Pattern: 8
Pick Pattern: 8

Moderately fast

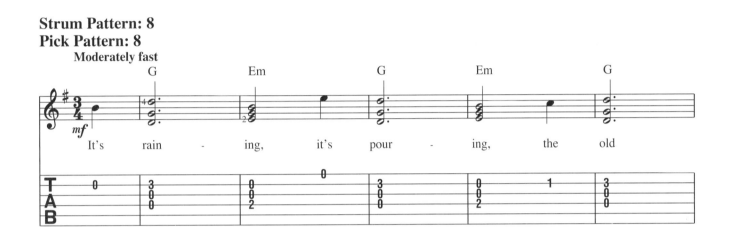

It's rain - ing, it's pour - ing, the old

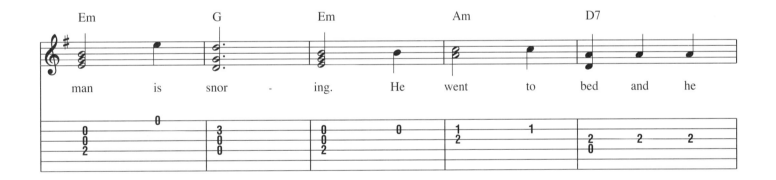

man is snor - ing. He went to bed and he

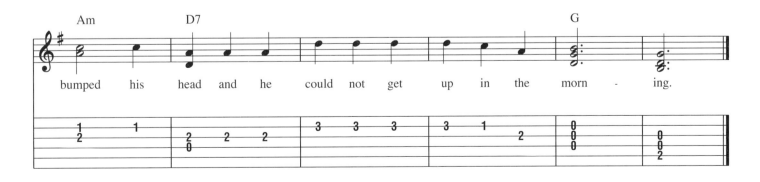

bumped his head and he could not get up in the morn - ing.

Jack and Jill

Traditional

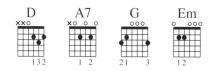

Strum Pattern: 8
Pick Pattern: 8

Verse
Moderately fast

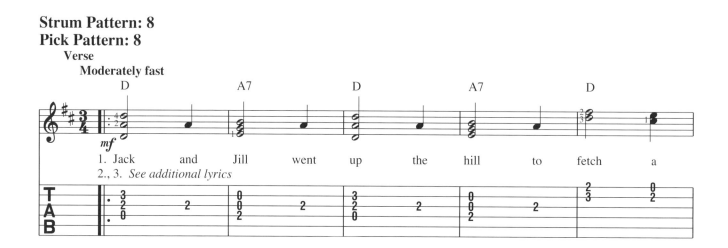

1. Jack and Jill went up the hill to fetch a
2., 3. *See additional lyrics*

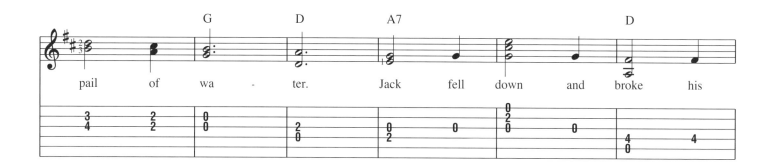

pail of wa - ter. Jack fell down and broke his

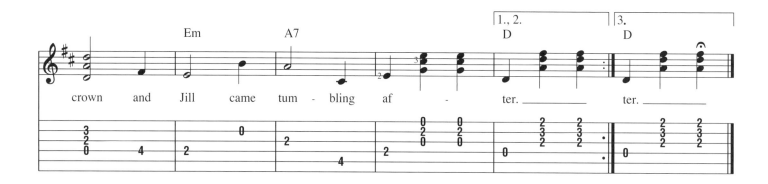

crown and Jill came tum - bling af - ter. _____ ter. _____

Additional Lyrics

2. Up Jack got and home did trot,
   As fast as he could caper.
   Went to bed to mend his head
   With vinegar and brown paper.

3. Jill came in and she did grin
   To see his paper plaster.
   Mother vexed, did whip her next
   For causing Jack's disaster.

Jack Be Nimble

Traditional

Strum Pattern: 4
Pick Pattern: 1

Jesus Loves Me

Words by Anna B. Warner
Music By William B. Bradbury

Strum Pattern: 3
Pick Pattern: 3

Additional Lyrics

2. Jesus, take this heart of mine,
   Make it pure and wholly Thine.
   Thou hast bled and died for me,
   I will henceforth live for Thee.

3. Jesus loves me; He who died,
   Heaven's gate to open wide.
   He will wash away my sin,
   Let His little child come in.

Kum Ba Yah

Traditional Spiritual

Strum Pattern: 4
Pick Pattern: 1, 2

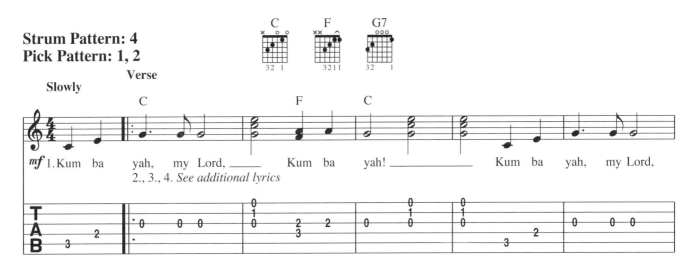

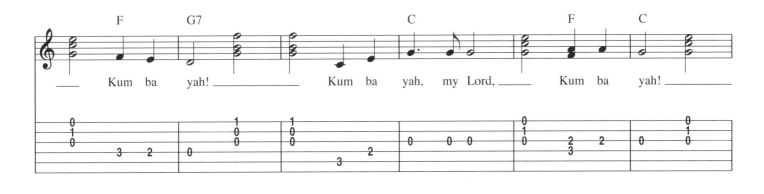

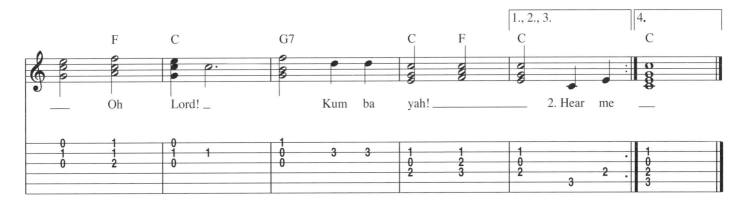

Additional Lyrics

2. Hear me crying, Lord, Kum ba yah!
   Hear me crying, Lord, Kum ba yah!
   Hear me crying, Lord, Kum ba yah!
   Oh Lord! Kum ba yah!

3. Hear me praying, Lord, Kum ba yah!
   Hear me praying, Lord, Kum ba yah!
   Hear me praying, Lord, Kum ba yah!
   O Lord! Kum ba yah!

4. Oh I need you, Lord, Kum ba yah!
   Oh I need you, Lord, Kum ba yah!
   Oh I need you, Lord, Kum ba yah!
   Oh Lord! Kum ba yah!

Knicky Knacky Knocky Noo

Traditional

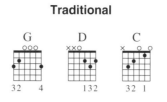

Strum Pattern: 8
Pick Pattern: 8

Verse
Moderately fast

1. With my hands on my head, what have I here?

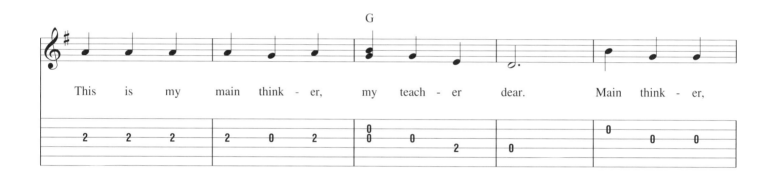

This is my main think - er, my teach - er dear. Main think - er,

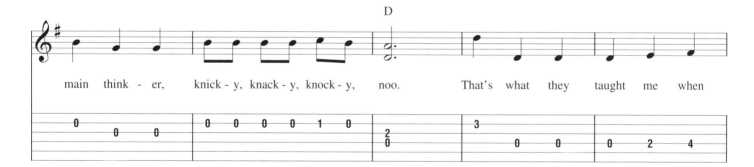

main think - er, knick - y, knack - y, knock - y, noo. That's what they taught me when

I went to school. 2. With my hands on my eyes, what have I

3. - 10. See additional lyrics

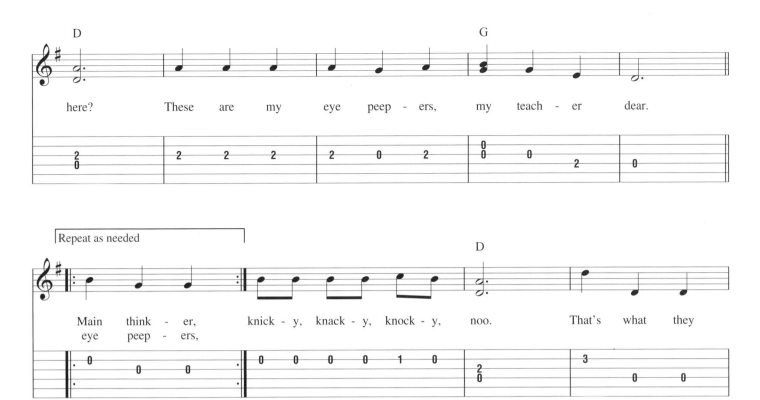

here? These are my eye peep - ers, my teach - er dear.

Repeat as needed

Main think - er, knick - y, knack - y, knock - y, noo. That's what they
eye peep - ers,

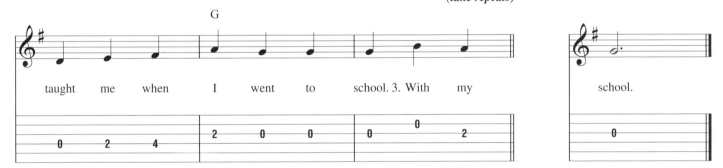

9th time, To Coda ⊕   *1st-7th times, D.S.*   ⊕ **Coda**
                         8th time, D.S. al Coda
                         (take repeats)

taught me when I went to school. 3. With my   school.

Additional Lyrics

3. With my hands on my nose,
   What have I here?
   This is my smell boxer, my teacher dear.
   Main thinker, eye peepers, smell boxer,
   Knicky, knacky, knocky, noo.
   That's what they taught me when I went to school.

4. With my hands on my mouth,
   What have I here?
   This is my chatterboxer, my teacher dear.
   Main thinker, eye peepers, smell boxer, chatterboxer,
   Knicky, knacky, knocky, noo.
   That's what they taught me when I went to school.

5. With my hands on my chin,
   What have I here?
   This is my chin wagger, my teacher dear.
   Main thinker, eye peepers, smell boxer, chatterboxer,
   Chin wagger, knicky, knacky, knocky, noo.
   That's what they taught me when I went to school.

6. With my hands on my chest,
   What have I here?
   This is my air blower, my teacher dear.
   Main thinker, eye peepers, smell boxer, chatterboxer,
   Chin wagger, air blower, knicky, knacky, knocky, noo.
   That's what they taught me when I went to school.

7. With my hands on my stomach,
   What have I here?
   This is my bread basket, my teacher dear.
   Main thinker, eye peepers, smell boxer, chatterboxer,
   Chin wagger, air blower, bread basket,
   Knicky, knacky, knocky, noo.
   That's what they taught me when I went to school.

8. With my hands on my lap,
   What have I here?
   This is my lap sitter, my teacher dear.
   Main thinker, eye peepers, smell boxer, chatterboxer,
   Chin wagger, air blower, bread basket, lap sitter,
   Knicky, knacky, knocky, noo.
   That's what they taught me when I went to school.

9. With my hands on my knees,
   What have I here?
   These are my knee knockers, my teacher dear.
   Main thinker, eye peepers, smell boxer, chatterboxer,
   Chin wagger, air blower, bread basket, lap sitter,
   Knee knockers, knicky, knacky, knocky, noo.
   That's what they taught me when I went to school.

10. With my hands on my feet,
    What have I here?
    These are my toe tappers, my teacher dear.
    Main thinker, eye peepers, smell boxer, chatterboxer,
    Chin wagger, air blower, bread basket, lap sitter,
    Knee knockers, toe tappers, knicky, knacky, knocky, noo.
    That's what they taught me when I went to school.

Ladybird, Ladybird

Traditional

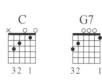

Strum Pattern: 8
Pick Pattern: 8

Intro
Moderately slow

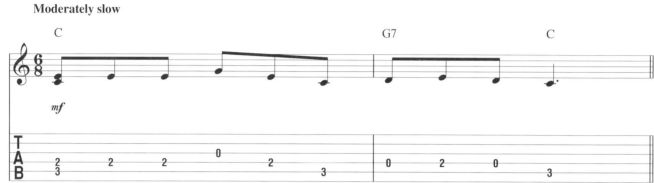

Verse

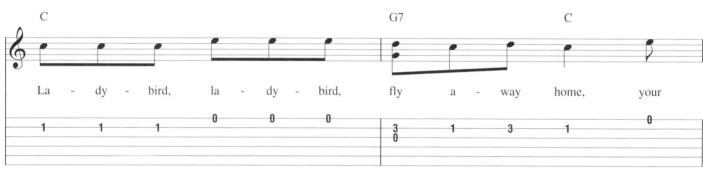

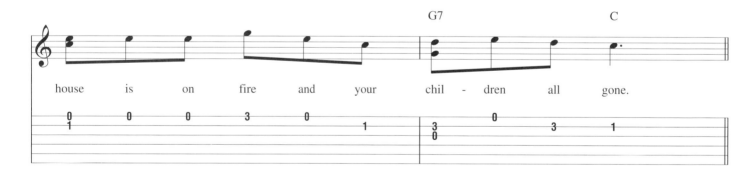

Outro

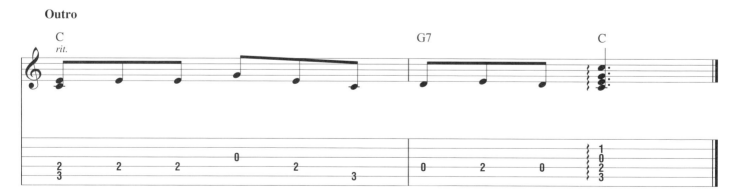

Lavender's Blue

English Folk Song

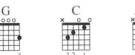

Strum Pattern: 8
Pick Pattern: 8

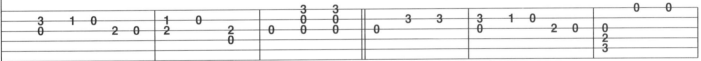

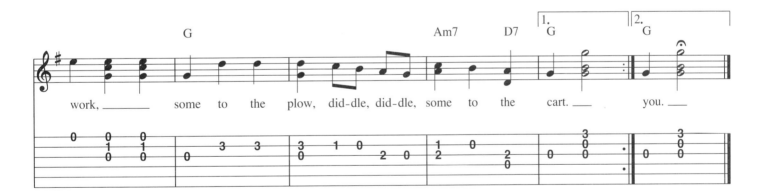

Additional Lyrics

3. Some to make hay, diddle, diddle,
   Some to cut corn,
   While you and I, diddle, diddle,
   Keep ourselves warm.

4. Lavender's green, diddle, diddle,
   Lavender's blue,
   If you love me, diddle, diddle,
   I will love you.

Lazy Katy, Will You Get Up?

Traditional

Strum Pattern: 8
Pick Pattern: 8

Additional Lyrics

2. No, Mother, I won't get up,
   Won't get up, won't get up.
   No, Mother, I won't get up
   This cold and frosty morning.

3. What if I give you some bread and jam,
   Bread and jam, bread and jam?
   What if I give you some bread and jam
   This cold and frosty morning?

4. No, Mother, I won't get up,
   Won't get up, won't get up.
   No, Mother, I won't get up
   This cold and frosty morning.

5. What if I give you some bacon and eggs,
   Bacon and eggs, bacon and eggs?
   What if I give you some bacon and eggs
   This cold and frosty morning?

6. No, Mother, I won't get up,
   Won't get up, won't get up.
   No, Mother, I won't get up
   This cold and frosty morning.

7. What if I give you a crack on the head,
   Crack on the head, crack on the head?
   What if I give you a crack on the head
   This cold and frosty morning?

8. Yes, Mother, I will get up,
   Will get up, will get up.
   Yes, Mother, I will get up
   This cold and frosty morning.

Little Bo-Peep

Traditional

Strum Pattern: 8
Pick Pattern: 8

Verse
Moderately, in 2

1. Lit - tle Bo - Peep has lost her sheep and can't ___ tell where ___ to
2. – 5. *See additional lyrics*

find ___ them. ___ Leave them a - lone and they'll ___ come home, ___

wag - ging their tails ___ be - hind ___ them. ___ prop - er - ly placed. ___

Additional Lyrics

2. Little Bo Peep fell fast asleep,
   And dreamt she heard them bleating.
   But when she awoke, she found it a joke,
   For still they all were fleeting.

3. Then up she took her little crook,
   Determined for to find them.
   She found them indeed, but it made her heart bleed,
   For they'd left all their tails behind them!

4. It happened one day, as Bo Peep did stray
   Unto a meadow hard by.
   There she espied their tails, side by side,
   All hung on a tree to dry.

5. She heaved a sigh and wiped her eye,
   And over the hillocks she raced.
   And tried what she could, as a shepherdess should,
   That each tail should be properly placed.

Little Bird, Little Bird

Traditional

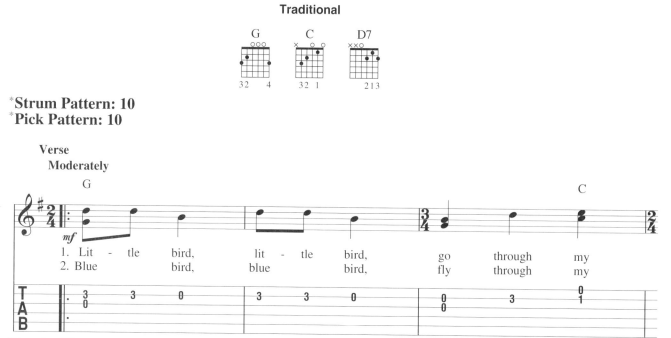

*Strum Pattern: 10
*Pick Pattern: 10

Verse
Moderately

*Use pattern 8 for meas.

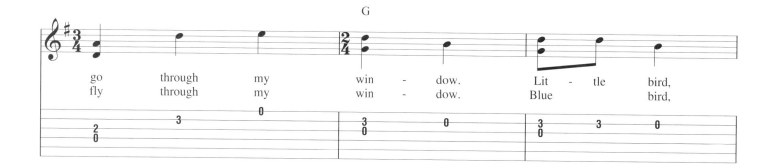

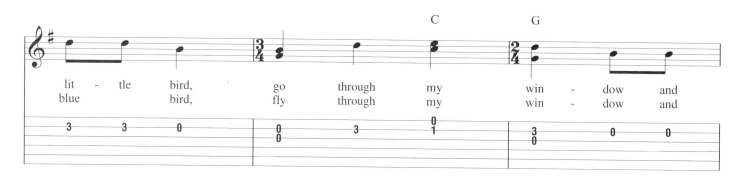

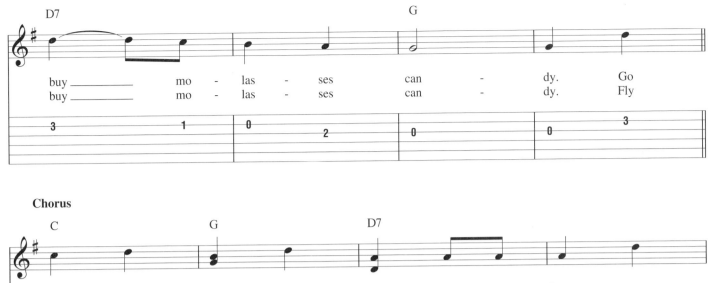

Chorus

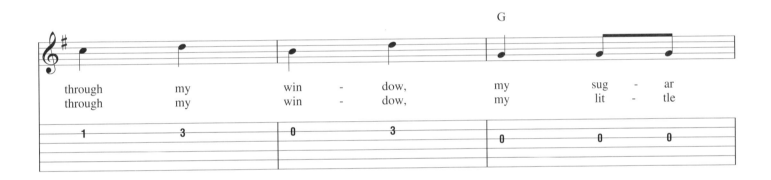

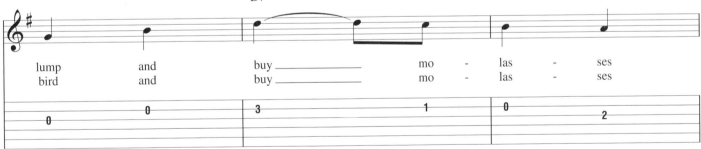

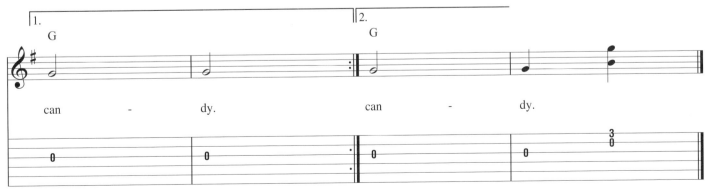

Little Boy Blue

Traditional

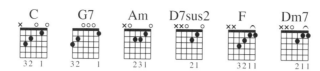

Strum Pattern: 7
Pick Pattern: 7

Moderately

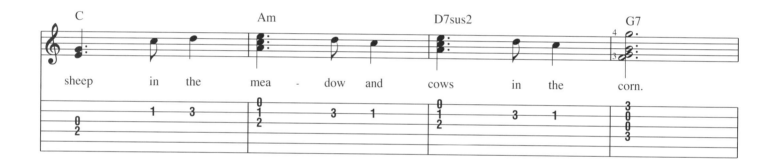

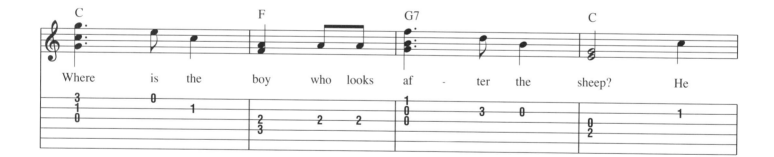

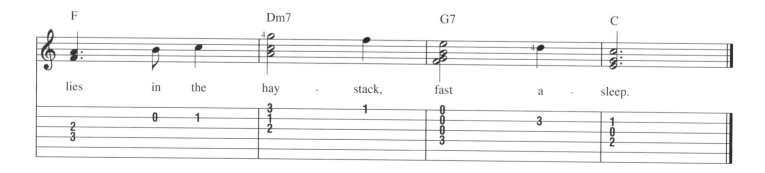

Little Girl

Traditional

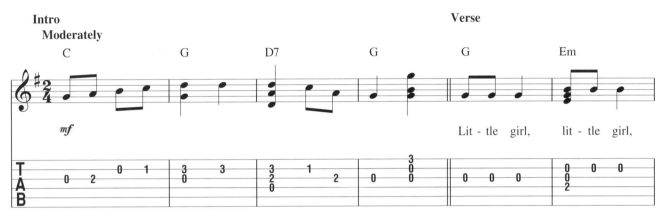

Strum Pattern: 10
Pick Pattern: 10

Intro
Moderately

Verse

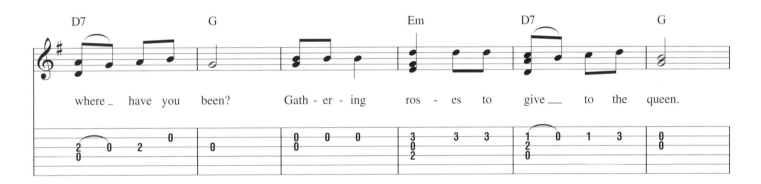

Lit - tle girl, lit - tle girl,

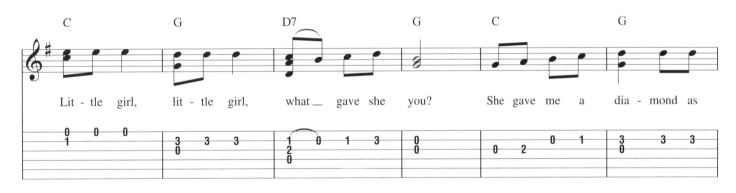

where _ have you been? Gath - er - ing ros - es to give _ to the queen.

Lit - tle girl, lit - tle girl, what _ gave she you? She gave me a dia - mond as

Outro

big as my shoe.

Little Jack Horner

Traditional

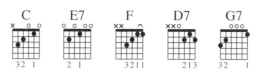

Strum Pattern: 8
Pick Pattern: 8

Moderately

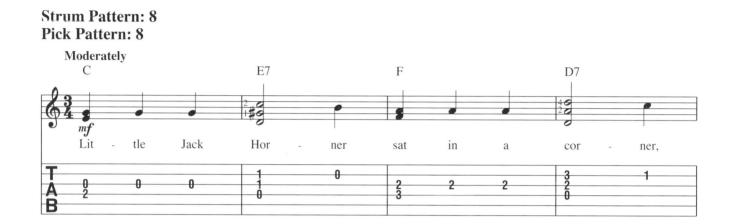

Lit - tle Jack Hor - ner sat in a cor - ner,

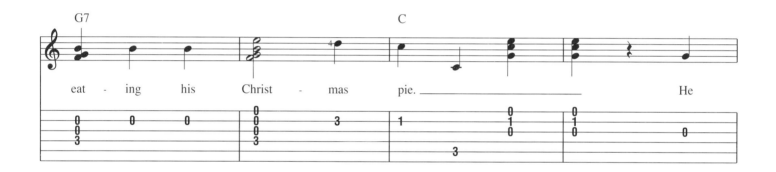

eat - ing his Christ - mas pie. _____ He

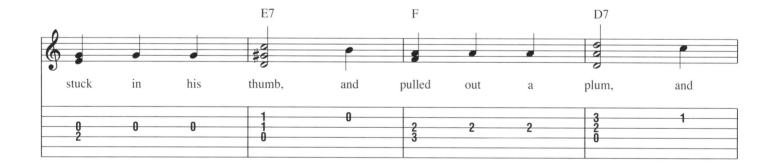

stuck in his thumb, and pulled out a plum, and

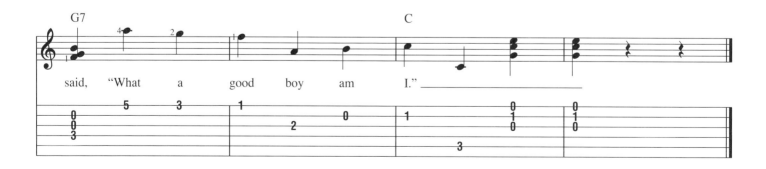

said, "What a good boy am I." _____

Little Miss Muffet

Traditional

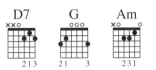

Strum Pattern: 8
Pick Pattern: 8

Brightly

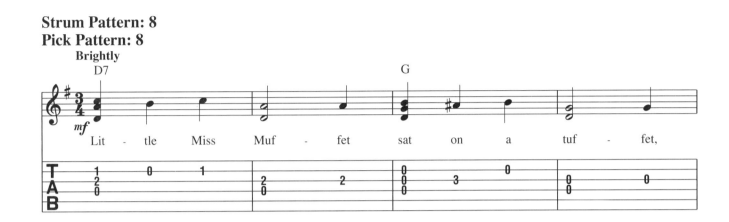

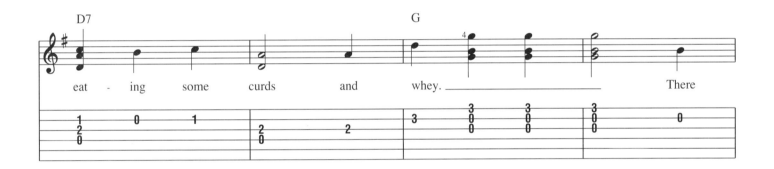

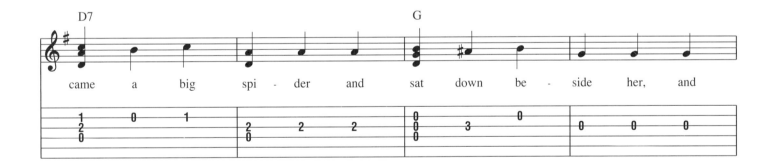

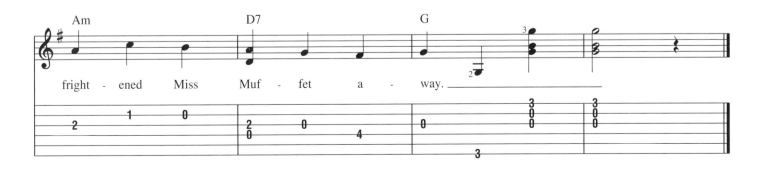

Little Polly Flinders

Traditional

Strum Pattern: 3
Pick Pattern: 3

Verse
Moderately

Lit - tle Pol - ly Flin - ders sat a - mong the cin - ders,

warm - ing her pret - ty lit - tle toes. Her

moth - er came and caught her and smacked her lit - tle daugh - ter for

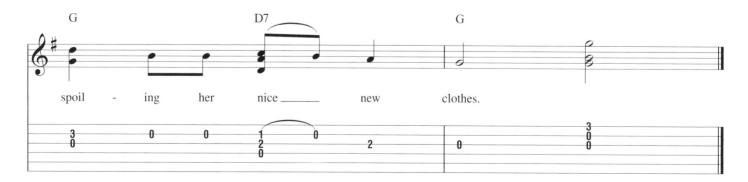

spoil - ing her nice _____ new clothes.

Little Tommy Tucker

Traditional

Strum Pattern: 7
Pick Pattern: 7

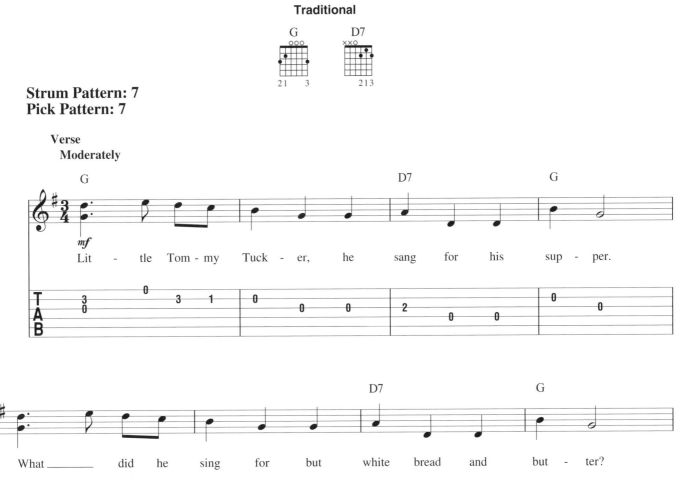

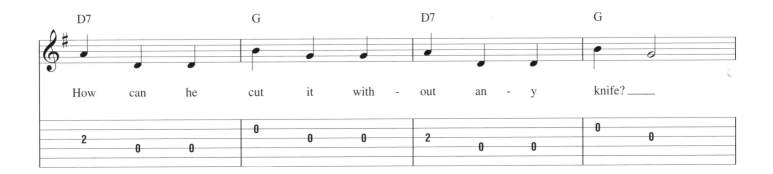

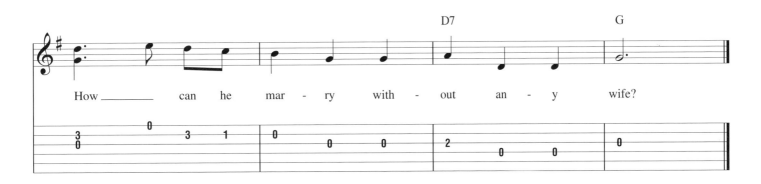

London Bridge Is Falling Down

Traditional

Strum Pattern: 3
Pick Pattern: 3

Additional Lyrics

2. Build it up with iron bars,
   Iron bars, iron bars.
   Build it up with iron bars,
   My fair lady.

3. Iron bars will bend and break,
   Bend and break, bend and break.
   Iron bars will bend and break,
   My fair lady.

4. Build it up with pins and needles,
   Pins and needles, pins and needles.
   Build it up with pins and needles,
   My fair lady.

5. Pins and needles rust and bend,
   Rust and bend, rust and bend.
   Pins and needles rust and bend,
   My fair lady.

6. Build it up with penny loaves,
   Penny loaves, penny loaves.
   Build it up with penny loaves,
   My fair lady.

7. Penny loaves will tumble down,
   Tumble down, tumble down.
   Penny loaves will tumble down,
   My fair lady.

8. Build it up with gold and silver,
   Gold and silver, gold and silver.
   Build it up with gold and silver,
   My fair lady.

9. Gold and silver I've not got,
   I've not got, I've not got.
   Gold and silver, I've not got,
   My fair lady.

10. Here's a prisoner I have got,
    I have got, I have got.
    Here's a prisoner I have got,
    My fair lady.

11. What's the prisoner done to you,
    Done to you, done to you?
    What's the prisoner done to you,
    My fair lady?

12. Stole my watch and broke my chain,
    Broke my chain, broke my chain.
    Stole my watch and broke my chain,
    My fair lady.

13. What'll you take to set him free,
    Set him free, set him free?
    What'll you take to set him free,
    My fair lady.

14. One hundred pounds will set him free,
    Set him free, set him free.
    One hundred pounds will set him free,
    My fair lady.

15. One hundred pounds we have not got,
    Have not got, have not got.
    One hundred pounds we have not got,
    My fair lady.

16. Then off to prison he must go,
    He must go, he must go.
    Then off to prison he must go,
    My fair lady.

London's Burning

Traditional

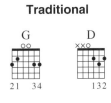

Strum Pattern: 8
Pick Pattern: 8

Verse
Moderately

1. Lon - don's (2.) burn - ing, Lon - don's burn - ing. Fetch the en - gines, fetch the

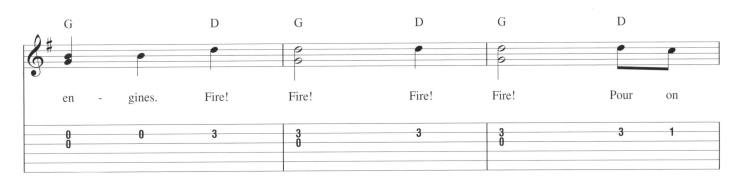

en - gines. Fire! Fire! Fire! Fire! Pour on

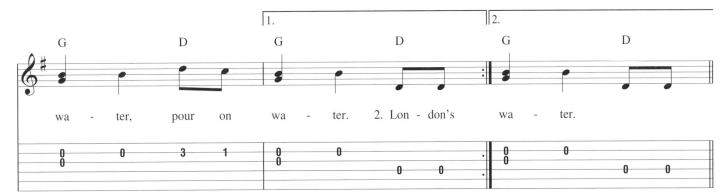

wa - ter, pour on wa - ter. 2. Lon - don's wa - ter.

Outro

Lucy Locket

Traditional Play Party

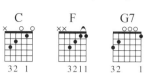

Strum Pattern: 10
Pick Pattern: 10

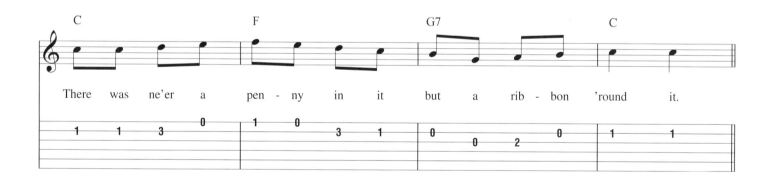

Mary Had a Little Lamb

Words by Sarah Josepha Hale

Traditional Music

Strum Pattern: 4
Pick Pattern: 4

Additional Lyrics

3. He followed her to school one day,
   School one day, school one day.
   He followed her to school one day,
   Which was against the rule.

4. It made the children laugh and play,
   Laugh and play, laugh and play.
   It made the children laugh and play,
   To see a lamb at school.

Mary, Mary, Quite Contrary

Traditional

Strum Pattern: 4
Pick Pattern: 4

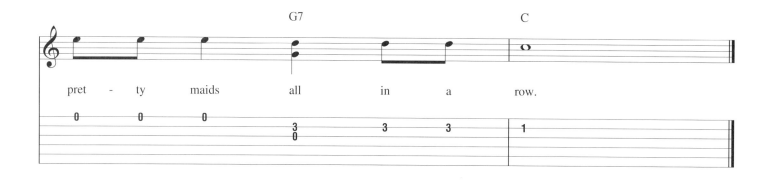

Merrily We Roll Along

Traditional

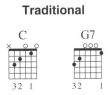

Strum Pattern: 3
Pick Pattern: 3

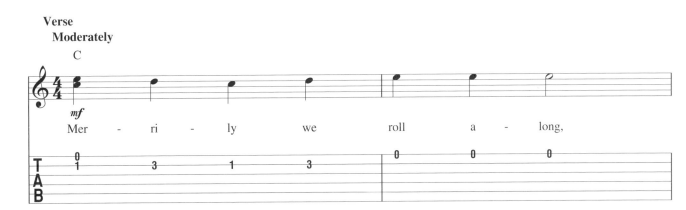

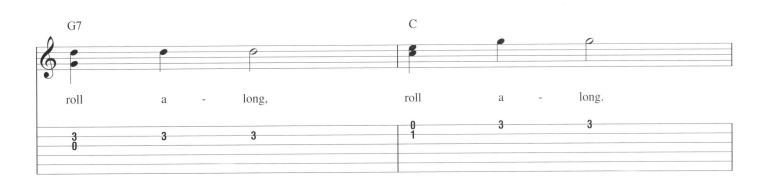

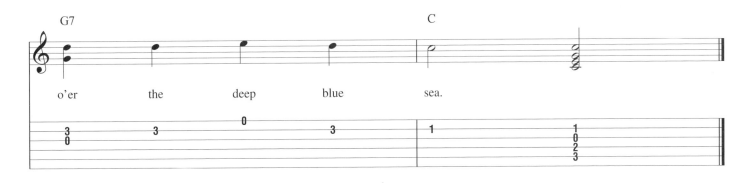

Michael Finnegan

Traditional

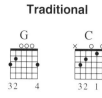

Strum Pattern: 3
Pick Pattern: 3

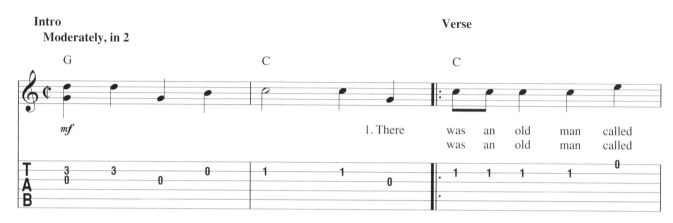

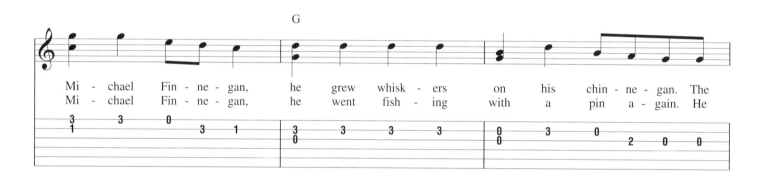

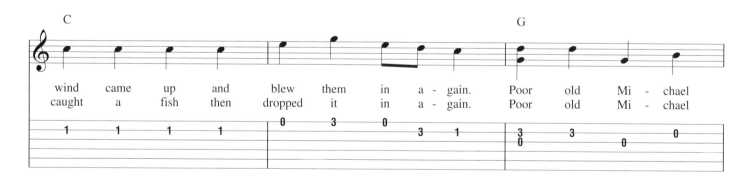

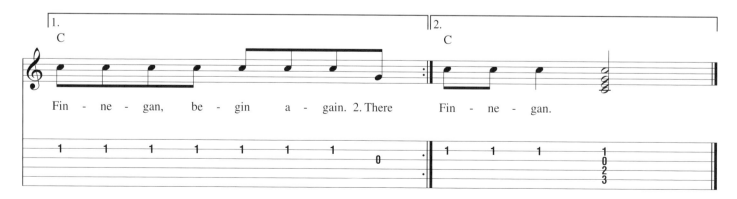

Michael Row the Boat Ashore

Traditional Folksong

Strum Pattern: 3
Pick Pattern: 3

Additional Lyrics

2. Jordan River is chilly and cold, hallelujah.
   Kills the body but not the soul, halleljah.

3. Jordan River is deep and wide, hallelujah.
   Milk and honey on the other side, hallelujah.

Miss Polly Had a Dolly

Traditional

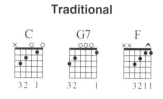

Strum Pattern: 5
Pick Pattern: 4

Verse

Moderately

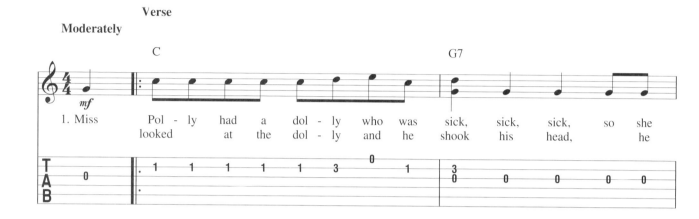

1. Miss Pol - ly had a dol - ly who was sick, sick, sick, so she
looked at the dol - ly and he shook his head, she

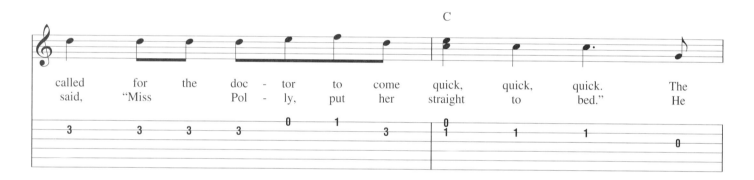

called for the doc - tor to come quick, quick, quick. The
said, "Miss Pol - ly, put her straight to bed." He

doc - tor came ___ with his bag, and his hat, and he
wrote on the pa - per for a pill, pill, pill, "I'll be

knocked ___ on the door ___ with a rat - a - tat tat. 2. He bill, bill, bill."
back ___ in the morn - ing with my

The Muffin Man

Traditional

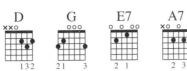

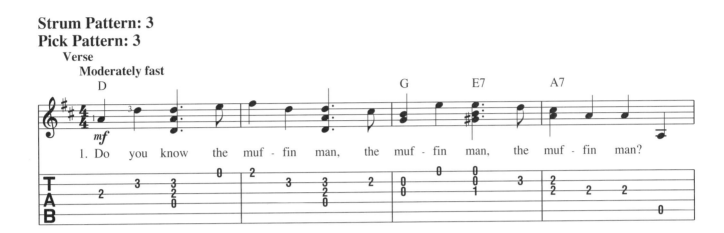

Strum Pattern: 3
Pick Pattern: 3

Verse
Moderately fast

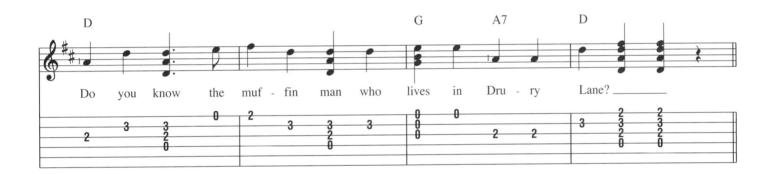

1. Do you know the muf-fin man, the muf-fin man, the muf-fin man?

Do you know the muf-fin man who lives in Dru-ry Lane?

Verse

2. Yes, we know the muf-fin man, the muf-fin man, the muf-fin man.

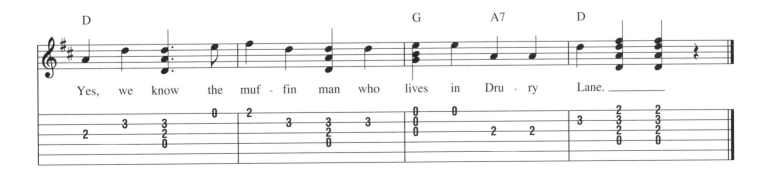

Yes, we know the muf-fin man who lives in Dru-ry Lane.

The Mulberry Bush

Traditional

Strum Pattern: 8
Pick Pattern: 8

Chorus
Lively

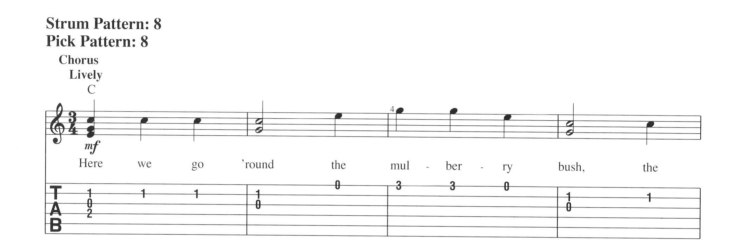

Here we go 'round the mul-ber-ry bush, the

mul-ber-ry bush, the mul-ber-ry bush.

Here we go 'round the mul-ber-ry bush so

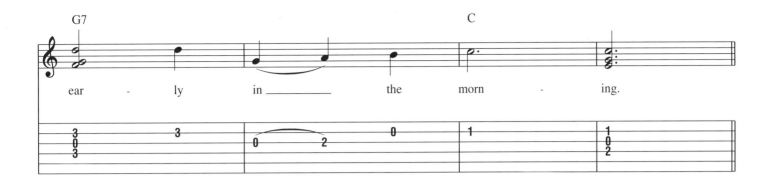

ear - ly in the morn - ing.

Verse

This is the way we wash our clothes, we wash our

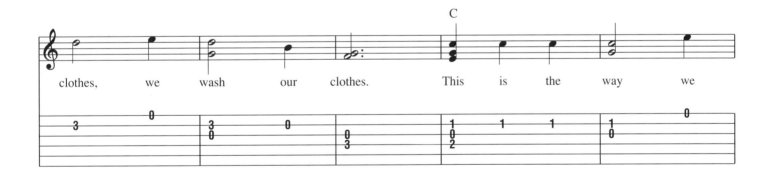

clothes, we wash our clothes. This is the way we

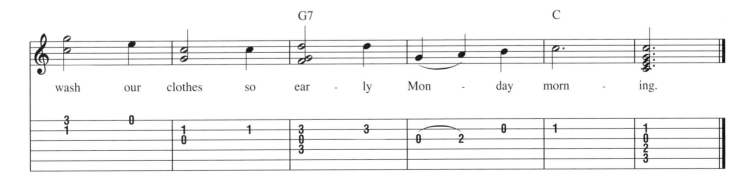

wash our clothes so ear - ly Mon - day morn - ing.

The Music Man

Traditional

Strum Pattern: 10
Pick Pattern: 10

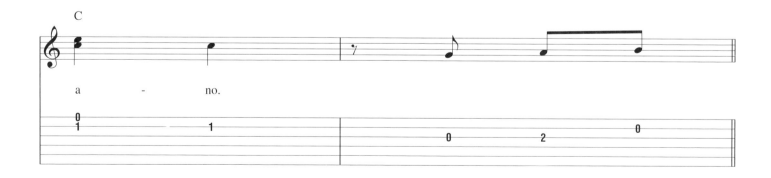

Bridge

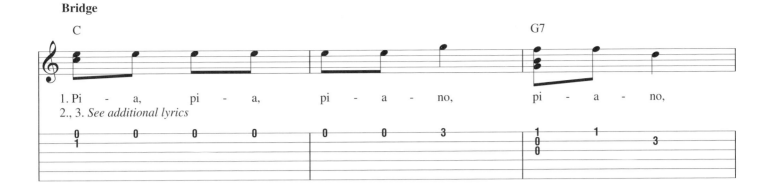

1. Pi - a, pi - a, pi - a - no, pi - a - no,
2., 3. *See additional lyrics*

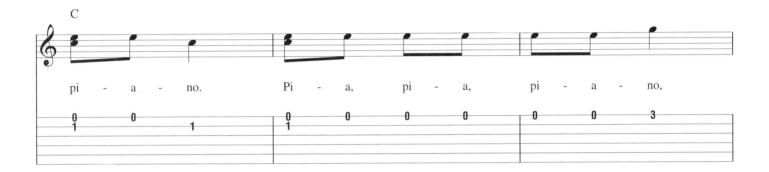

pi - a - no. Pi - a, pi - a, pi - a - no,

Repeat Bridge as needed, then D.C.
Last time, Fine

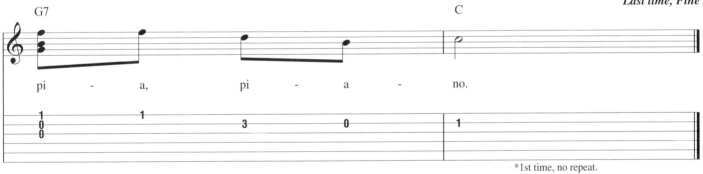

pi - a, pi - a - no.

*1st time, no repeat.

Additional Lyrics

2. I am the music man,
   I come from far away,
   And I can play.
   What can you play?
   I play the bass drum.

   Bridge 2 Boom-di, boom-di, boom-di-boom,
   Boom-di-boom, boom-di-boom.
   Boom-di, boom-di, boom-di-boom,
   Boom-di, boom-di-boom.
   Pi-a, pi-a, pi-a-no,
   Pi-a-no, pi-a-no.
   Pi-a, pi-a, pi-a-no,
   Pi-a, pi-a-no.

3. I am the music man,
   I come from far away,
   And I can play.
   What can you play?
   I play the trumpet.

   Bridge 3 Toot-ti, toot-ti, toot-ti-toot,
   Toot-ti-toot, toot-ti-toot.
   Toot-ti, toot-ti, toot-ti-toot,
   Toot-ti, toot-ti-toot.
   Boom-di, boom-di, boom-di-boom,
   Boom-di-boom, boom-di-boom.
   Boom-di, boom-di, boom-di-boom,
   Boom-di, boom-di-boom.
   Pi-a, pi-a, pi-a-no,
   Pi-a-no, pi-a-no.
   Pi-a, pi-a, pi-a-no,
   Pi-a, pi-a-no.

My Hat It Has Three Corners

Traditional

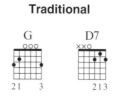

Strum Pattern: 8
Pick Pattern: 8

Verse
Moderately slow, in 2

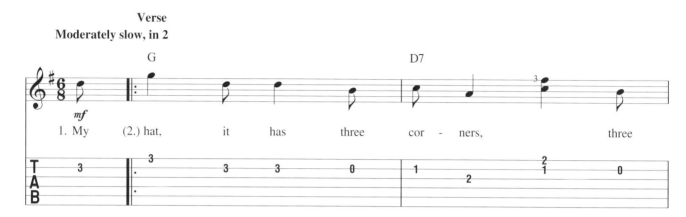

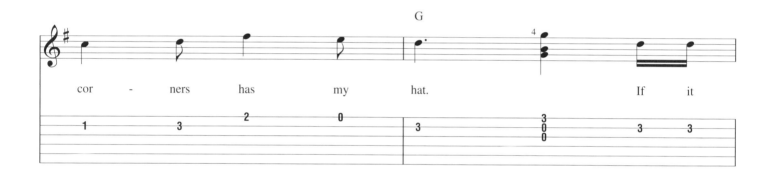

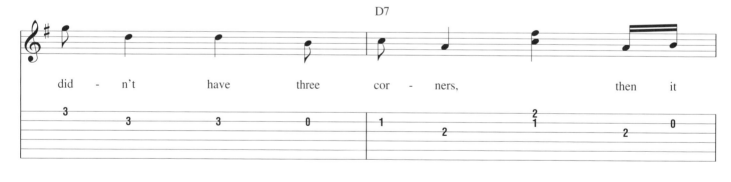

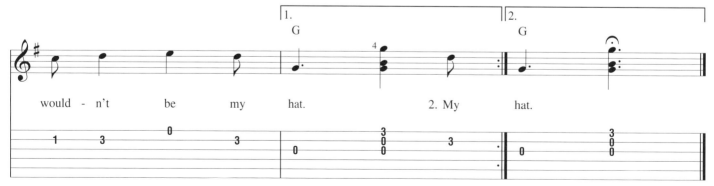

My Lady's Garden

Traditional

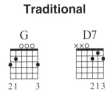

Strum Pattern: 8
Pick Pattern: 8

Intro
Moderately

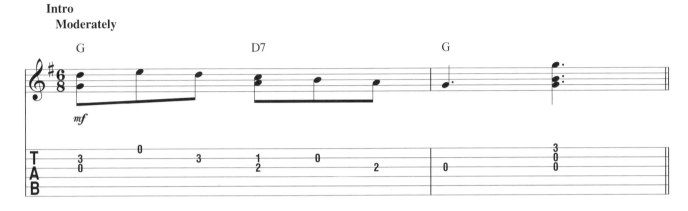

Verse

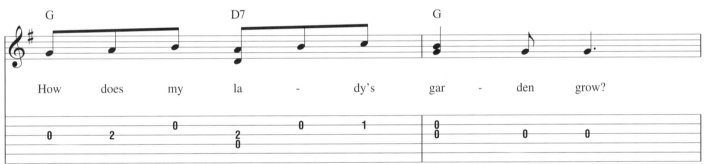

How does my la - dy's gar - den grow?

How does my la - dy's gar - den grow? With sil - ver bells and

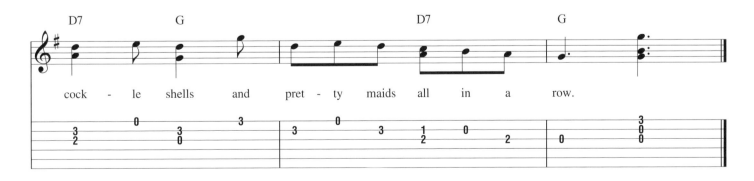

cock - le shells and pret - ty maids all in a row.

Nobody Loves Me

Traditional

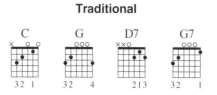

Strum Pattern: 3
Pick Pattern: 3

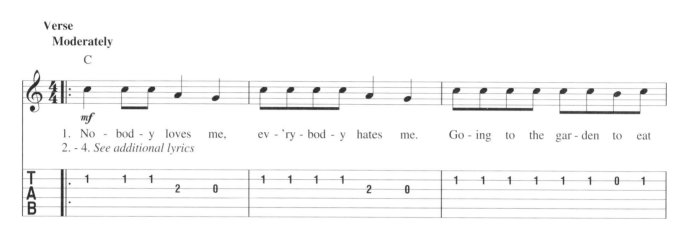

Additional Lyrics

2. Bite their heads of, suck their juice out,
   Throw their skins away.
   I don't see how birds can live on
   Worms three times a day.

3. Nobody loves me, ev'rybody hates me,
   Going to the garden to eat worms.
   Long, thin, slimy ones, short, fat, juicy ones,
   Gooey, gooey, gooey, gooey worms.

4. Long, thin, slimy ones slip down easily,
   Short, fat, juicy ones stick,
   Short, fat, juicy ones stick between your teeth,
   And the juice goes slurp, slurp, slurp.

The North Wind Doth Blow

Traditional

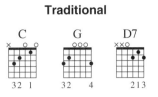

Strum Pattern: 7
Pick Pattern: 7

Verse
Moderately

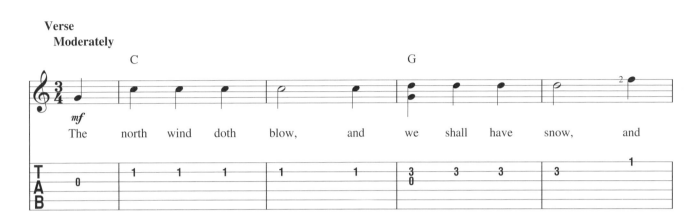

The north wind doth blow, and we shall have snow, and

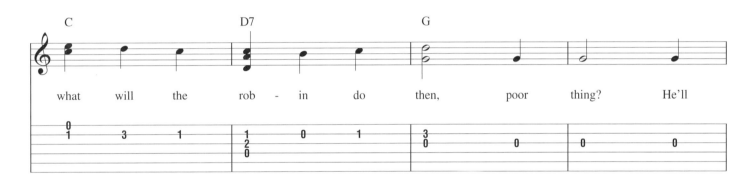

what will the rob - in do then, poor thing? He'll

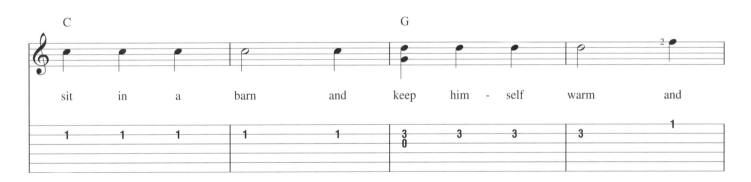

sit in a barn and keep him - self warm and

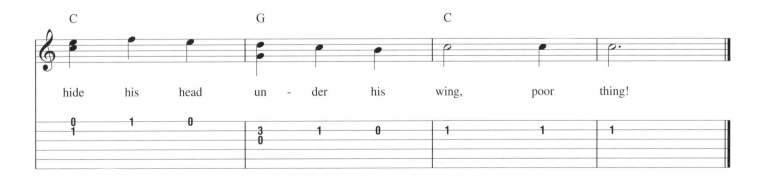

hide his head un - der his wing, poor thing!

Now I Lay Me Down to Sleep

Traditional

Strum Pattern: 3
Pick Pattern: 3

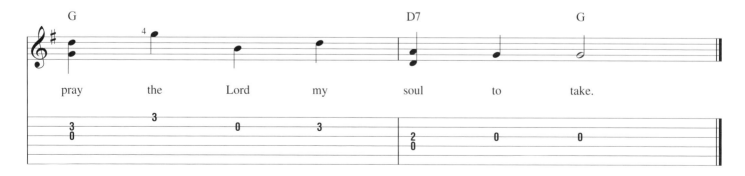

Now the Day Is Over

Words by Sabine Baring-Gould
Music by Joseph Barnby

Oh Dear!
What Can the Matter Be?

Traditional

Strum Pattern: 8
Pick Pattern: 8

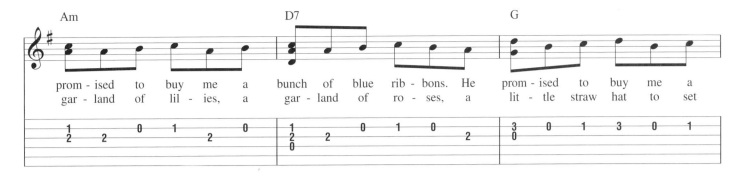

prom - ised to buy me a bunch of blue rib - bons. He prom - ised to buy me a
gar - land of lil - ies, a gar - land of ro - ses, a lit - tle straw hat to set

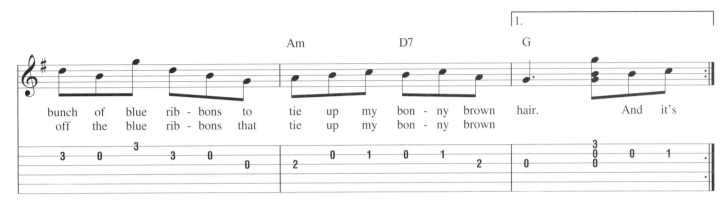

1.

bunch of blue rib - bons to tie up my bon - ny brown hair. And it's
off the blue rib - bons that tie up my bon - ny brown

2.

Outro-Chorus

hair. And it's oh dear! What can the mat - ter be?

Oh dear! What can the mat - ter be? Oh dear!

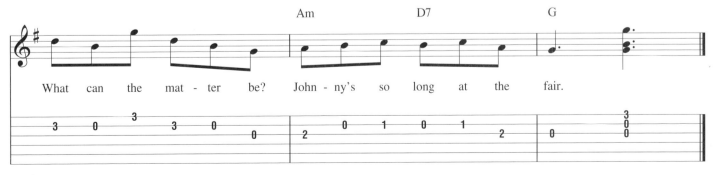

What can the mat - ter be? John - ny's so long at the fair.

Oh, We Can Play on the Big Bass Drum

Traditional

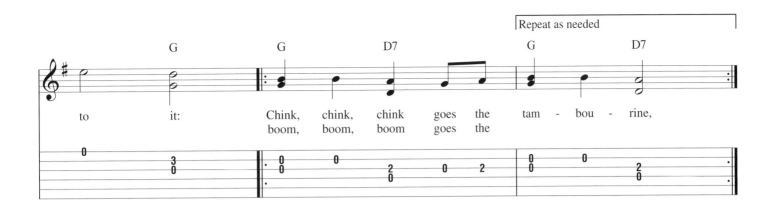

Repeat as needed

to it: Chink, chink, chink goes the tam - bou - rine,
boom, boom, boom goes the

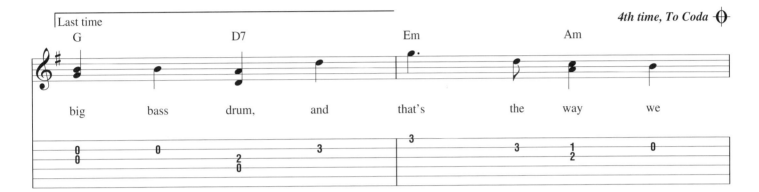

Last time

4th time, To Coda

big bass drum, and that's the way we

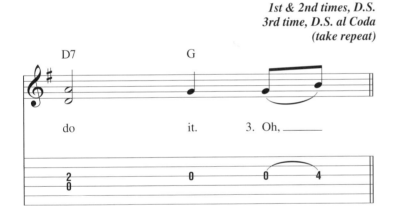

1st & 2nd times, D.S.
3rd time, D.S. al Coda
(take repeat)

do it. 3. Oh, _____

Coda

do it.

Additional Lyrics

3. Oh, we can play on the castanets,
   And this is the music to it:
   Click, clickety-click go the castanets,
   Chink, chink, chink goes the tambourine,
   Boom, boom, boom goes the big bass drum,
   And that's the way we do it.

4. Oh, we can play on the triangle,
   And this is the music to it:
   Ping, ping, ping goes the triangle,
   Click, clickety-click go the castanets,
   Chink, chink, chink goes the tambourine,
   Boom, boom, boom goes the big bass drum,
   And that's the way we do it.

5. Oh, we can play on the old banjo,
   And this is the music to it:
   Tum, tum, tum goes the old banjo,
   Ping, ping, ping goes the triangle,
   Click, clickety-click go the castanets,
   Chink, chink, chink goes the tambourine,
   Boom, boom, boom goes the big bass drum,
   And that's the way we do it.

Oh Where, Oh Where
Has My Little Dog Gone

Words by Sep. Winner
Traditional Melody

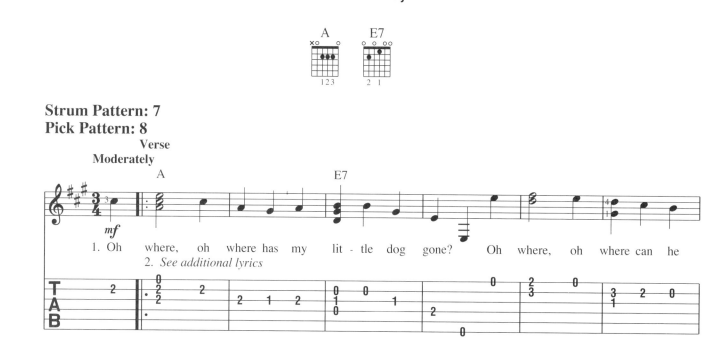

Strum Pattern: 7
Pick Pattern: 8

Verse
Moderately

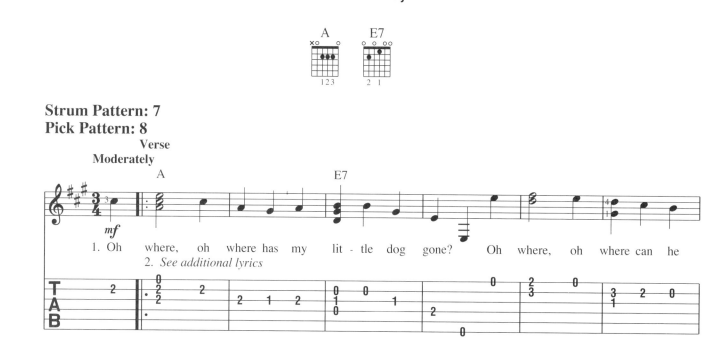

1. Oh where, oh where has my lit - tle dog gone? Oh where, oh where can he

2. See additional lyrics

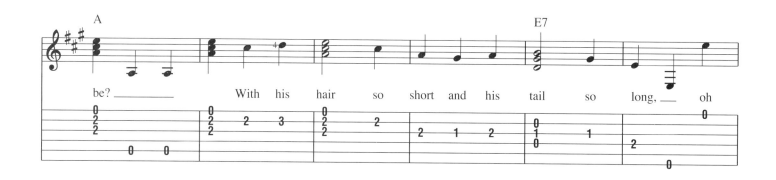

be? _____ With his hair so short and his tail so long, __ oh

where, oh where can he be? _____ 2. Oh me? _____

Additional Lyrics

2. Oh where, oh where has my little dog gone?
Oh where, oh where can he be?
If you see him anywhere, won't you please
Bring back my doggie to me?

Old King Cole

Traditional

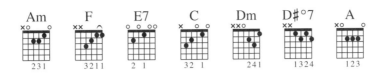

Strum Pattern: 3, 2
Pick Pattern: 3, 4

Moderately

Old King Cole was a mer-ry old __ soul, and a mer-ry old soul was he. _____ He __

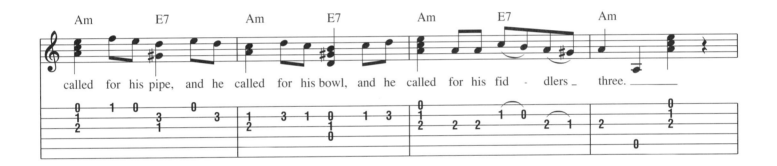

called for his pipe, and he called for his bowl, and he called for his fid - dlers _ three. _____

Ev - 'ry _ fid - dler _ had a fid-dle fine __ and a ver - y fine _ fid-dle had he. _____ Tweed-le

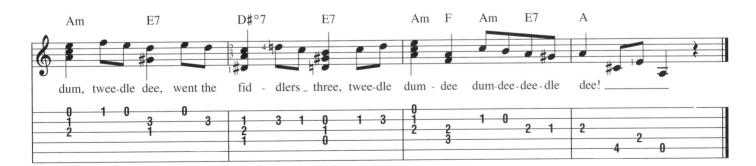

dum, twee-dle dee, went the fid - dlers _ three, twee-dle dum - dee dum-dee-dee-dle dee! _____

Old Blue

19th Century American South

Strum Pattern: 10
Pick Pattern: 10

Chorus

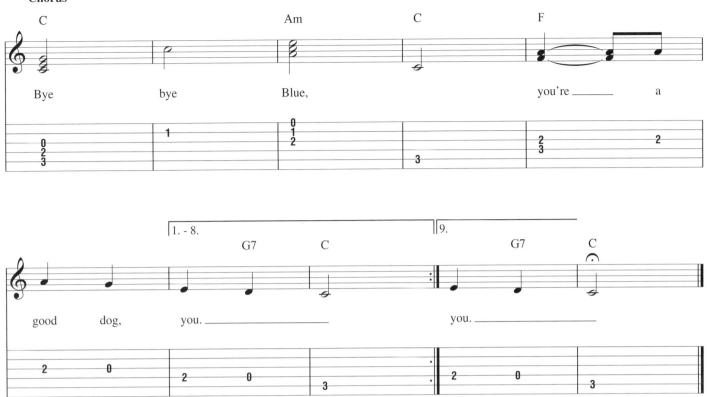

Additional Lyrics

2. Every night just about dark,
   Every night just about dark,
   Every night just about dark,
   Blue goes out and begins to bark.

3. Everything just in a rush,
   Everything just in a rush,
   Everything just in a rush,
   He treed a possum in a white-oak bush.

4. Possum walked out to the end of a limb.
   Possum walked out to the end of a limb.
   Possum walked out to the end of a limb.
   Blue set down and talked to him.

5. Blue got sick and very sick.
   Blue got sick and very sick.
   Blue got sick and very sick.
   Sent for the doctor to come here quick.

6. Doctor come and he come in a run.
   Doctor come and he come in a run.
   Doctor come and he come in a run,
   Says, "Old Blue, your hunting's done."

7. Blue, he died and died so hard.
   Blue, he died and died so hard.
   Blue, he died and died so hard,
   Scratched little holes all around the yard.

8. Laid him out in a shady place.
   Laid him out in a shady place.
   Laid him out in a shady place,
   Covered him o'er with a possum's face.

9, When I get to heaven, I'll tell you what I'll do,
   When I get to heaven, I'll tell you what I'll do,
   When I get to heaven, I'll tell you what I'll do,
   I'll take my horn and blow for Blue.

Old Davey Jones

Traditional

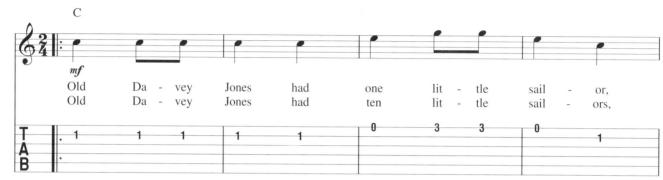

Strum Pattern: 10
Pick Pattern: 10

Chorus
Moderately

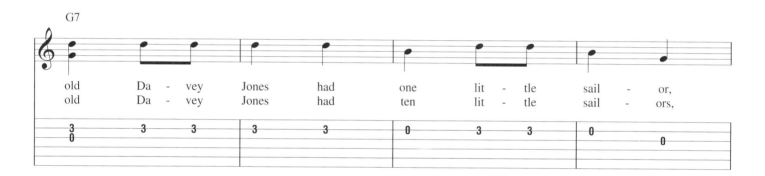

Old Da - vey Jones had one lit - tle sail - or,
Old Da - vey Jones had ten lit - tle sail - ors,

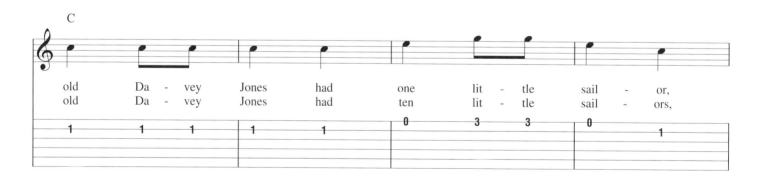

old Da - vey Jones had one lit - tle sail - or,
old Da - vey Jones had ten lit - tle sail - ors,

old Da - vey Jones had one lit - tle sail - or,
old Da - vey Jones had ten lit - tle sail - ors,

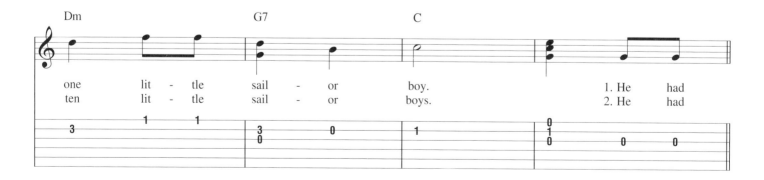

one lit - tle sail - or boy.
ten lit - tle sail - or boys.

1. He had
2. He had

Verse

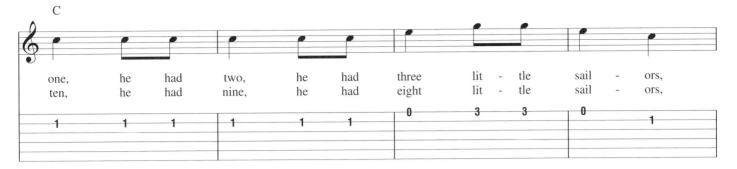

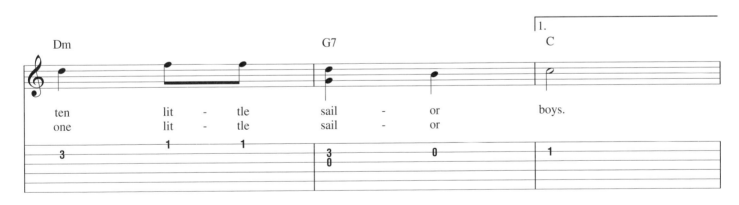

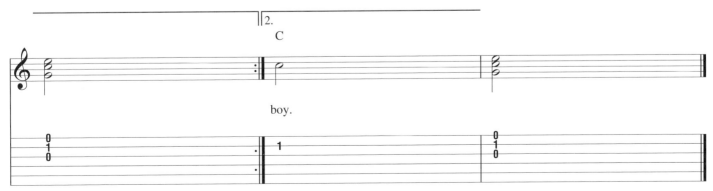

Old Hogan's Goat

Traditional

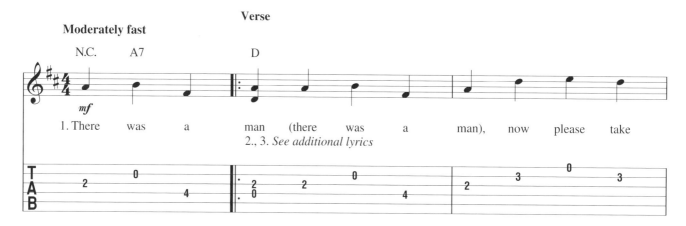

Strum Pattern: 2
Pick Pattern: 4

Verse

Moderately fast

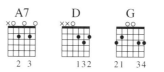

There was a man (there was a man), now please take
2., 3. *See additional lyrics*

note (now please take note), there was a man (there was a

man) who had a goat (who had a goat). He loved that

goat (he loved that goat), in - deed he did (in - deed he

did), he loved that goat (he loved that goat) just like a

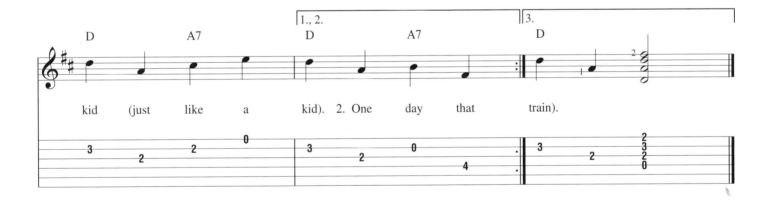

kid (just like a kid). 2. One day that train).

Additional Lyrics

2. One day that goat (one day that goat)
   Was feeling fine (was feeling fine),
   Ate three red shirts (ate three red shirts)
   From off the line (from off the line).
   The old man grabbed (the old man grabbed)
   Her by the back (her by the back)
   And tied her to (and tied her to)
   The railway track (the railway track).

3. Now when the train (now when the train)
   Came into sight (came into sight),
   The goat grew pale (the goat grew pale)
   And grey with fright (and grey with fright).
   She struggled hard (she struggled hard)
   And then again (and then again)
   Coughed up the shirts (coughed up the shirts)
   And flagged the train (and flagged the train).

Old MacDonald Had a Farm

Traditional Children's Song

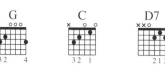

Strum Pattern: 2
Pick Pattern: 4

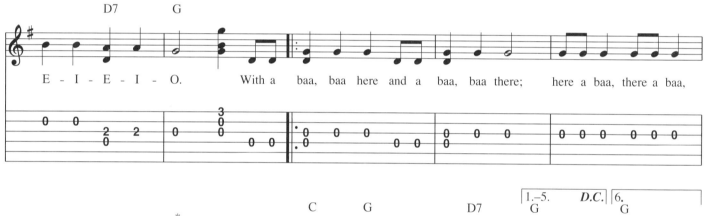

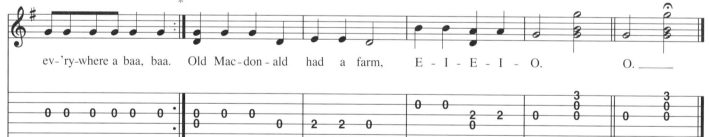

*Repeat as needed for each animal.

Additional Lyrics

2. Cows… moo, moo.

3. Pigs… oink, oink.

4. Ducks… quack, quack.

5. Chickens… cluck, cluck.

6. Turkeys… gobble, gobble.

On Top of Old Smoky

Kentucky Mountain Folksong

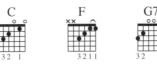

Strum Pattern: 8
Pick Pattern: 8

Additional Lyrics

2. Well, a-courting's a pleasure,
And parting is grief.
But a false-hearted lover
Is worse than a thief.

3. A thief he will rob you
And take all you have,
But a false-hearted lover
Will send you to your grave.

4. And the grave will decay you
And turn you to dust.
And where is the young man
A poor girl can trust?

5. They'll hug you and kiss you
And tell you more lies
Than the cross-ties on the railroad,
Or the stars in the skies.

6. They'll tell you they love you,
Just to give your heart ease.
But the minute your back's turned,
They'll court whom they please.

7. So come all you young maidens
And listen to me,
Never place your affection
On a green willow tree.

8. For the leaves they will wither
And the roots they will die.
And your true love will leave you,
And you'll never know why.

Old Mother Hubbard

Traditional

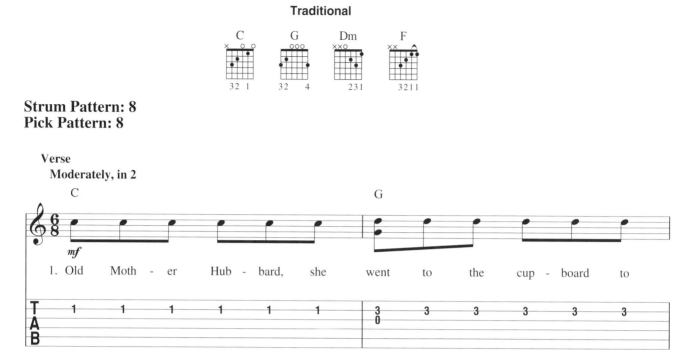

Strum Pattern: 8
Pick Pattern: 8

Verse
Moderately, in 2

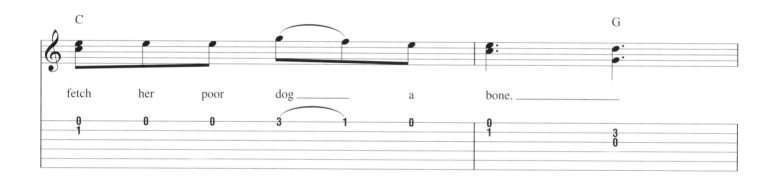

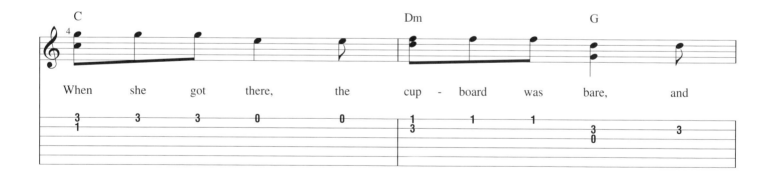

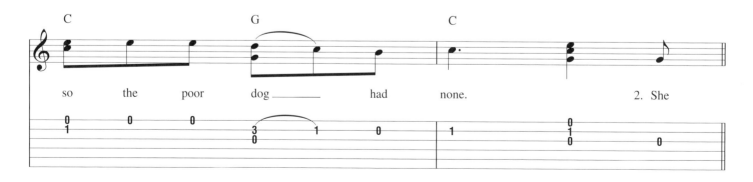

Verse

Additional Lyrics

3. She went to the undertaker's
   To buy him a coffin,
   But when she came back,
   The poor dog was laughing.

4. She took a clean dish
   To get him some tripe,
   But when she got back,
   He was smoking a pipe.

5. She went to the fishmonger's
   To buy him some fish,
   But when she came back,
   He was licking the dish.

6. She went to the tavern
   For white wine and red,
   But when she got back,
   The dog stood on his head.

7. She went to the fruiterer's
   To buy him some fruit,
   But when she came back,
   He was playing the flute.

8. She went to the tailor's
   To buy him a coat,
   But when she came back,
   He was riding a goat.

9. She went to the hatter's
   To buy him a hat,
   But when she came back,
   He was feeding the cat.

10. She went to the barber's
    To buy him a wig,
    But when she came back,
    He was dancing a jig.

11. She went to the cobbler's
    To buy him some shoes,
    But when she came back,
    He was reading the news.

12. She went to the seamstress
    To buy him some linen,
    But when she came back,
    The dog was a spinning.

13. She went to the hosier's
    To buy him some hose,
    But when she came back,
    He was dressed in his clothes.

14. The Dame made a curtsey,
    The dog made a bow,
    The Dame said, "Your servant,"
    The dog said, "Bow-wow."

One Elephant

Traditional

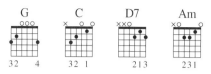

Strum Pattern: 3
Pick Pattern: 3

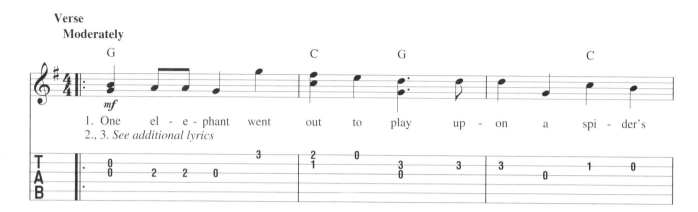

Verse
Moderately

1. One el - e - phant went out to play up - on a spi - der's
2., 3. *See additional lyrics*

web one day. He found it such e - nor - mous fun that he

called for an - oth - er el - e - phant to come. all fell down.

Additional Lyrics

2. Two elephants went out to play
   Upon a spider's web one day.
   He found it such enormous fun
   That he called for another elephant to come.

3. Three elephants went out to play
   Upon a spider's web one day.
   He found it such enormous fun
   But the web, it broke, and they all fell down.

One, Two, Three, Four, Five

Traditional Folk Song

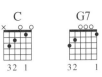

Strum Pattern: 10
Pick Pattern: 10

Verse
Moderately

1. One, two, three, four, five, once I caught a
2. Why did you let it go? Be - cause it bit my

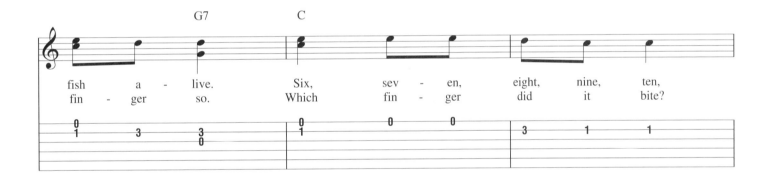

fish a - live. Six, sev - en, eight, nine, ten,
fin - ger so. Which fin - ger did it bite?

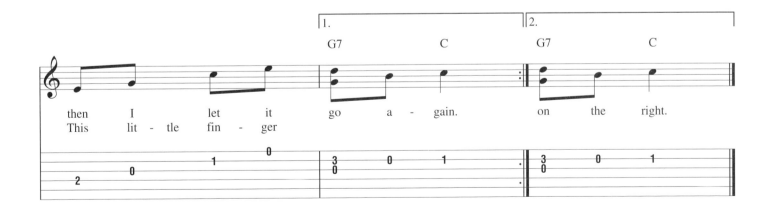

then I let it go a - gain.
This lit - tle fin - ger on the right.

One Finger, One Thumb

Traditional

Strum Pattern: 8
Pick Pattern: 8

Verse
Fast

1. One fin-ger, one thumb, keep mov - ing, one fin-ger, one

thumb, keep mov - ing, one fin-ger, one thumb, keep

mov - ing, we'll all be mer-ry and bright.

Repeat as needed

%. Verse

2. One fin - ger, one thumb, one mov - ing, one
arm, keep

3. - 6. See additional lyrics

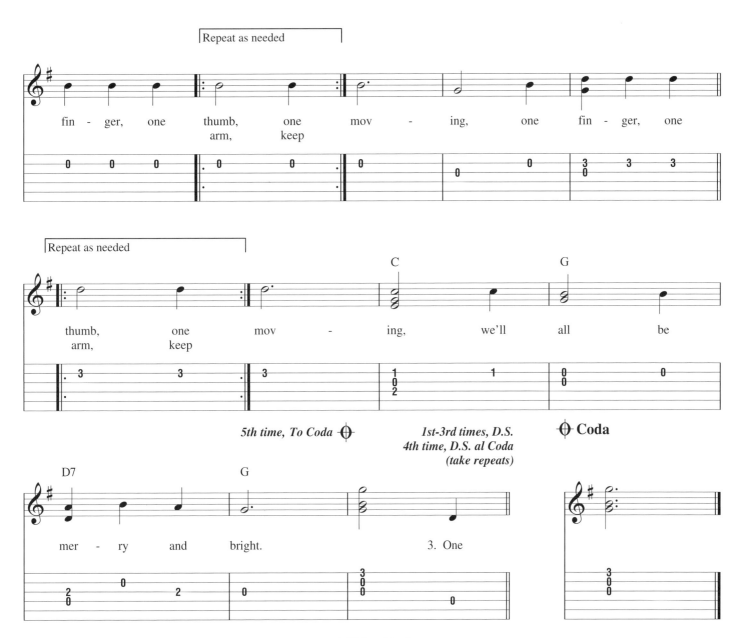

5th time, To Coda ⊕   *1st-3rd times, D.S.*
4th time, D.S. al Coda
(take repeats)   ⊕ **Coda**

Additional Lyrics

3. One finger, one thumb, one arm, one leg, keep moving,
One finger, one thumb, one arm, one leg, keep moving,
One finger, one thumb, one arm, one leg, keep moving,
We'll all be merry and bright.

4. One finger, one thumb, one arm, one leg,
One nod of the head, keep moving,
One finger, one thumb, one arm, one leg,
One nod of the head, keep moving,
One finger, one thumb, one arm, one leg,
One nod of the head, keep moving,
We'll all be merry and bright.

5. One finger, one thumb, one arm, one leg,
One nod of the head, stand up, sit down, keep moving,
One finger, one thumb, one arm, one leg,
One nod of the head, stand up, sit down, keep moving,
One finger, one thumb, one arm, one leg,
One nod of the head, stand up, sit down, keep moving,
We'll all be merry and bright.

6. One finger, one thumb, one arm, one leg,
One nod of the head, stand up, sit down,
Turn around, keep moving,
One finger, one thumb, one arm, one leg,
One nod of the head, stand up, sit down,
Turn around, keep moving,
One finger, one thumb, one arm, one leg,
One nod of the head, stand up, sit down,
Turn around, keep moving,
We'll all be merry and bright.

One Man Went to Mow

Traditional

Strum Pattern: 3
Pick Pattern: 3

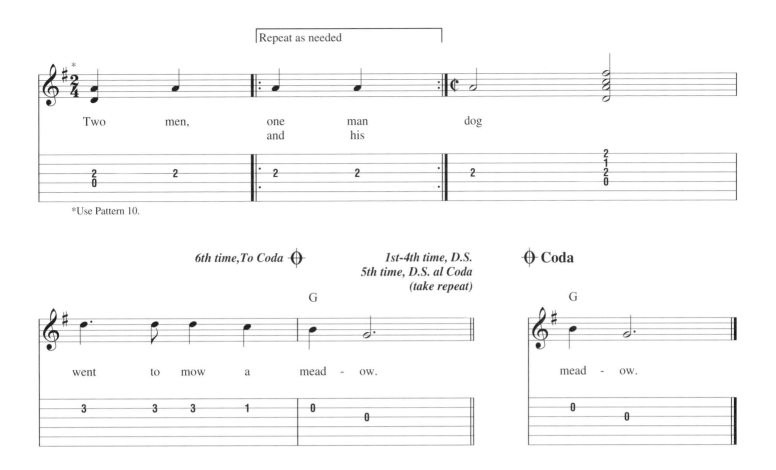

*Use Pattern 10.

6th time, To Coda ⊕   *1st-4th time, D.S.*
                         5th time, D.S. al Coda
                              (take repeat)   ⊕ **Coda**

G   G

went   to   mow   a   mead - ow.   mead - ow.

Additional Lyrics

3. Three men went to mow,
   Went to mow a meadow.
   Three men, two men,
   One man and his dog
   Went to mow a meadow.

4. Four men went to mow,
   Went to mow a meadow.
   Four men, three men, two men,
   One man and his dog
   Went to mow a meadow.

5. Five men went to mow,
   Went to mow a meadow.
   Five men, four men, three men,
   Two men, one man and his dog
   Went to mow a meadow.

6. Six men went to mow,
   Went to mow a meadow.
   Six men, five men, four men,
   Three men, two men,
   One man and his dog
   Went to mow a meadow.

7. Seven men went to mow,
   Went to mow a meadow.
   Seven men, six men, five men,
   Four men, three men, two men,
   One man and his dog
   Went to mow a meadow.

8. Eight men went to mow,
   Went to mow a meadow.
   Eight men, seven men, six men,
   Five men, four men, three men,
   Two men, one man and his dog
   Went to mow a meadow.

9. Nine men went to mow,
   Went to mow a meadow.
   Nine men, eight men, seven men,
   Six men, five men, four men,
   Three men, two men,
   One man and his dog
   Went to mow a meadow.

10. Ten men went to mow,
    Went to mow a meadow.
    Ten men, nine men, eight men,
    Seven men, six men, five men,
    Four men, three men, two mcn,
    One man and his dog
    Went to mow a meadow.

One, Two Buckle My Shoe

Traditional

Strum Pattern: 8
Pick Pattern: 8

Oranges, Lemons

Traditional

Strum Pattern: 8
Pick Pattern: 8

Verse
Moderately

1., 2. "Or-an-ges and lem-ons," say the bells of Saint Clem-ent's. "You owe me five far-things," say the

bells of Saint Mar-tin's. "When will you pay me?" say the bells of Old Bai-ley.

"When I grow rich," say the bells at Shore-ditch. Here comes a can-dle to ___

light you to bed, and here comes a chop-per to ___ chop off your head.

The Owl and the Pussycat

Traditional

Strum Pattern: 8
Pick Pattern: 8

love - ly pus - sy! O pus - sy, my love, what a beau - ti - ful pus - sy you

are, you are, you are. What a

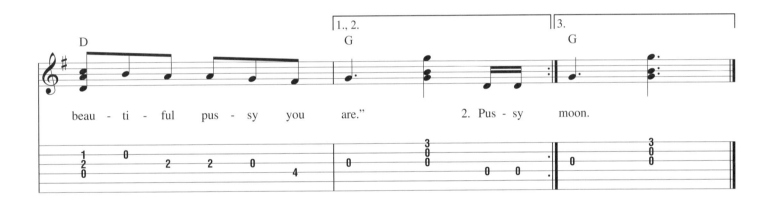

beau - ti - ful pus - sy you are." 2. Pus - sy moon.

Additional Lyrics

2. Pussy said to the owl, "You elegant fowl,
How charmingly sweet you sing!
Oh, let us be married; too long we have tarried.
But what shall we do for a ring?"
They sailed away for a year and a day
To the land where the bong tree grows.
And there in the woods, a piggy-wig stood
With a ring at the end of his nose,
His nose,
His nose,
With a ring at the end of his nose.

3. "Dear pig, are you willing to sell for one shilling
Your ring?" Said the piggy, "I will."
So they took it away and were married next day
By the turkey who lives on the hill.
They dined on mince and slices of quince,
Which they ate with a runcible spoon.
And hand in hand on the edge of the sand,
They danced by the light of the moon,
The moon,
The moon,
They danced by the light of the moon.

Pat-a-Cake

Traditional

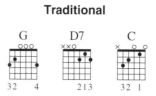

Strum Pattern: 8
Pick Pattern: 8

Verse
Moderately fast

Pat - a - cake, pat - a - cake, bak - er's man,

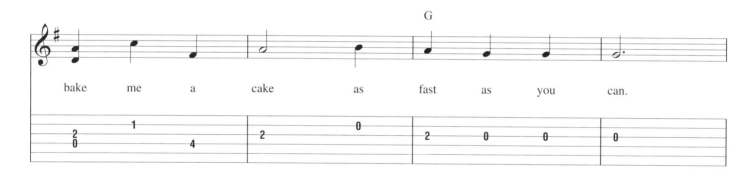

bake me a cake as fast as you can.

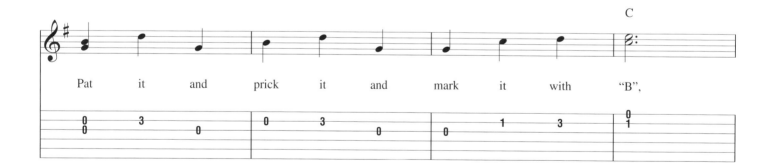

Pat it and prick it and mark it with "B",

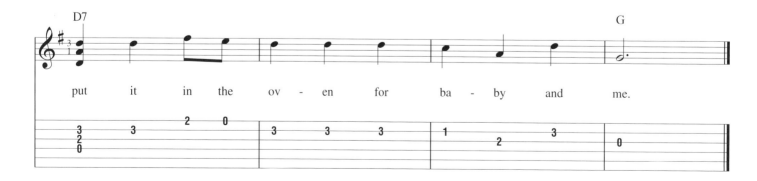

put it in the ov - en for ba - by and me.

Peanut Sat on a Railroad Track

Traditional

Strum Pattern: 3, 2
Pick Pattern: 3, 4

Moderately

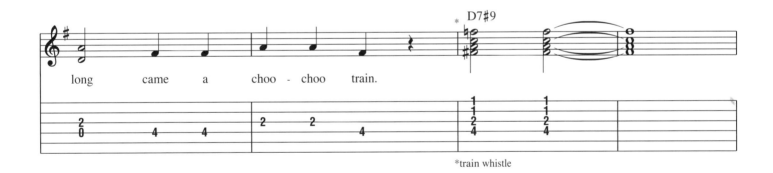

A pea - nut sat on a rail - road track, his heart was all a - flut - ter. A -

long came a choo - choo train.

*train whistle

Pea - nut ____ but - ter.

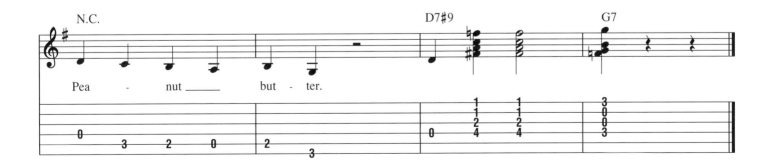

Pease Porridge Hot

Traditional

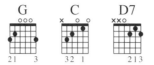

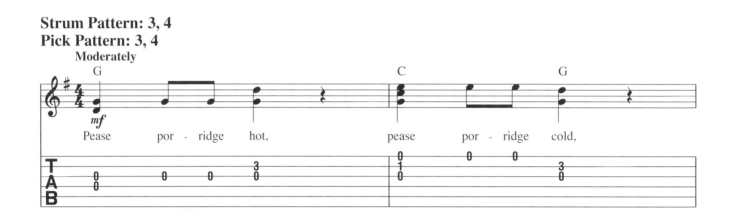

Strum Pattern: 3, 4
Pick Pattern: 3, 4

Moderately

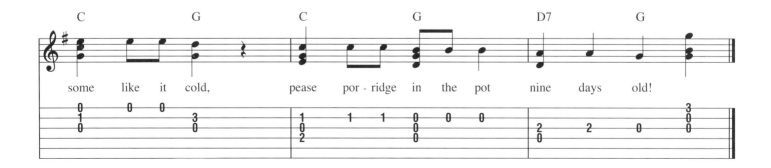

Peter Piper

Traditional

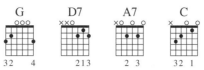

Strum Pattern: 3
Pick Pattern: 3

Verse
Moderately

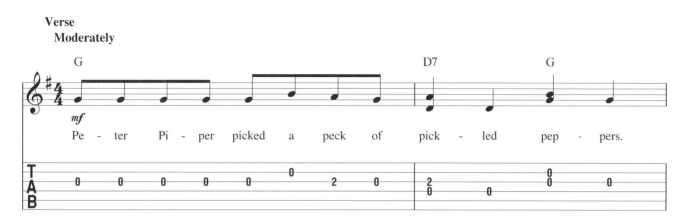

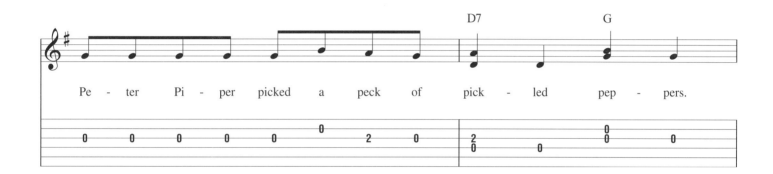

Pe - ter Pi - per picked a peck of pick - led pep - pers.

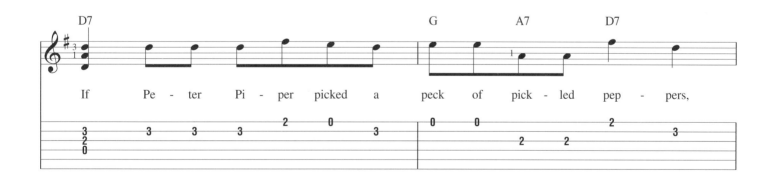

Pe - ter Pi - per picked a peck of pick - led pep - pers.

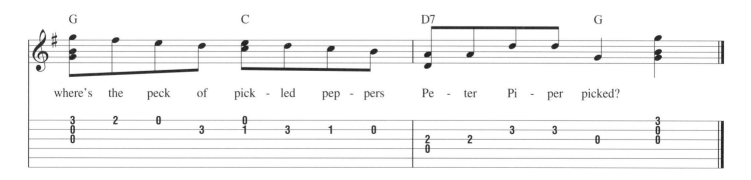

If Pe - ter Pi - per picked a peck of pick - led pep - pers,

where's the peck of pick - led pep - pers Pe - ter Pi - per picked?

Peter, Peter, Pumpkin Eater

Traditional

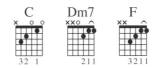

Strum Pattern: 4, 3
Pick Pattern: 3, 6

Moderately

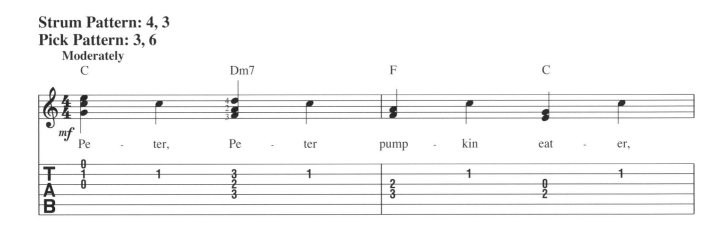

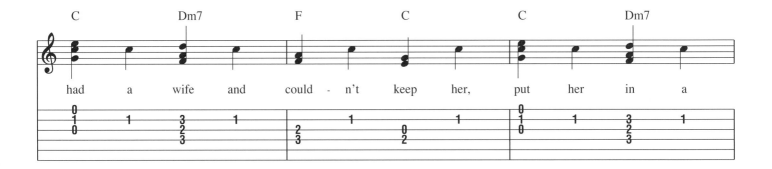

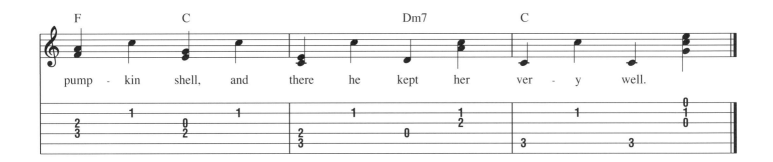

Polly Put the Kettle On

Traditional

Strum Pattern: 10
Pick Pattern: 10

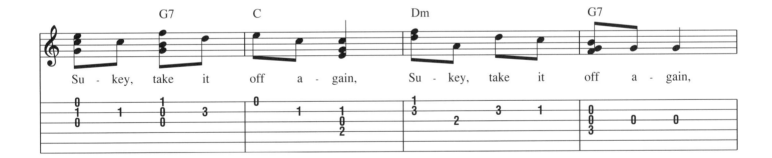

Polly Wolly Doodle

Traditional American Minstrel Song

Strum Pattern: 2
Pick Pattern: 4

Moderately fast

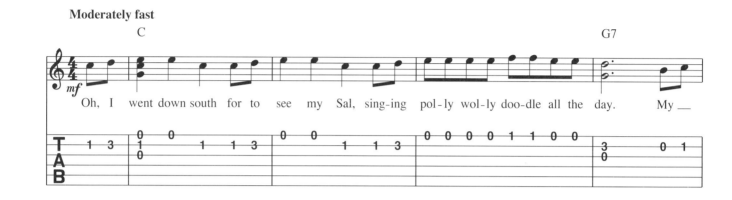

Oh, I went down south for to see my Sal, sing-ing pol-ly wol-ly doo-dle all the day. My —

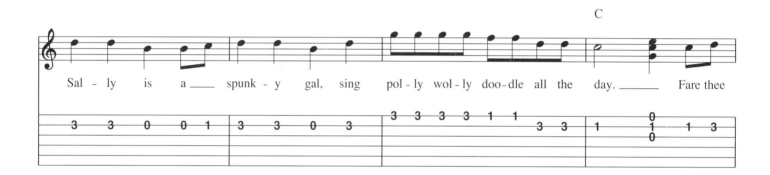

Sal-ly is a — spunk-y gal, sing pol-ly wol-ly doo-dle all the day. — Fare thee

well, fare thee well, fare thee well, my fair-y fay. For I'm goin' to Lou-'si-an-a for to

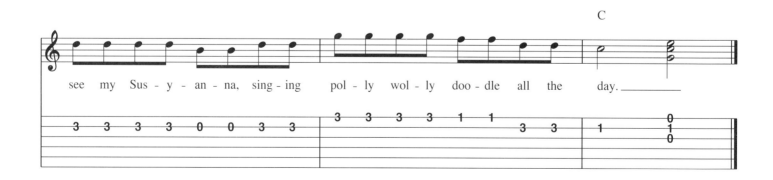

see my Sus-y-an-na, sing-ing pol-ly wol-ly doo-dle all the day. —

Pop Goes the Weasel

Traditional

Strum Pattern: 9
Pick Pattern: 7

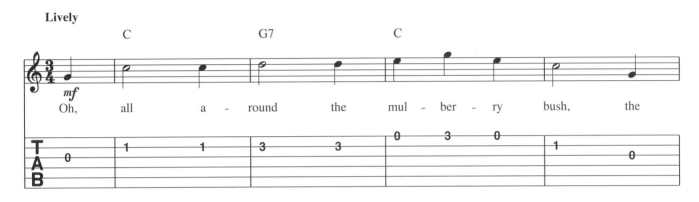

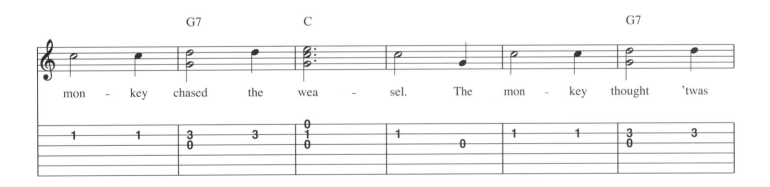

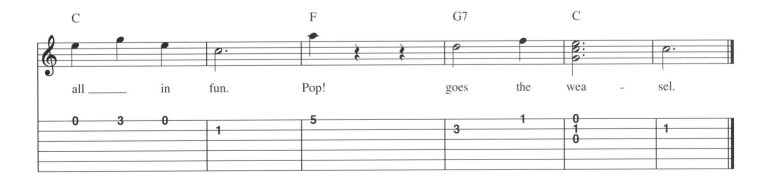

Pussy Cat

Traditional

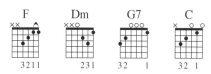

Strum Pattern: 8
Pick Pattern: 8

Intro
Moderately, in 2

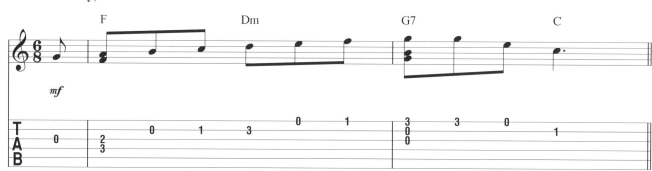

Verse

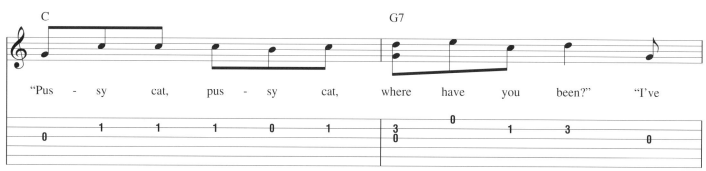

"Pus - sy cat, pus - sy cat, where have you been?" "I've

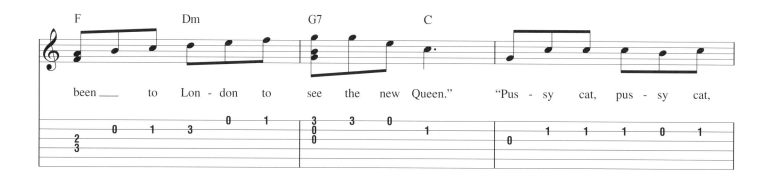

been ___ to Lon - don to see the new Queen." "Pus - sy cat, pus - sy cat,

what did you there?" "I caught ___ a lit - tle mouse un - der her chair."

The Rainbow Song

Traditional

Strum Pattern: 3
Pick Pattern: 3

The Quartermaster's Store

Traditional

Strum Pattern: 3
Pick Pattern: 3

Chorus

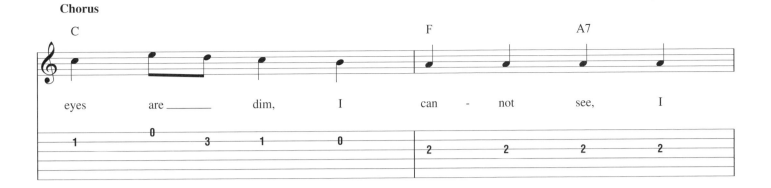

eyes are _____ dim, I can - not see, I

have not _____ brought my specs with me, I

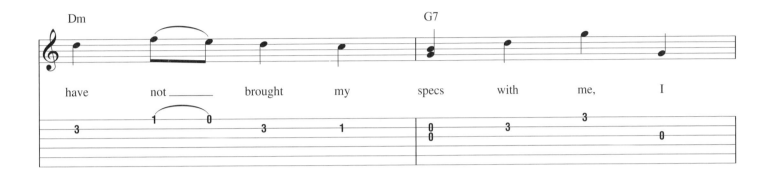

have not _____ brought my _____

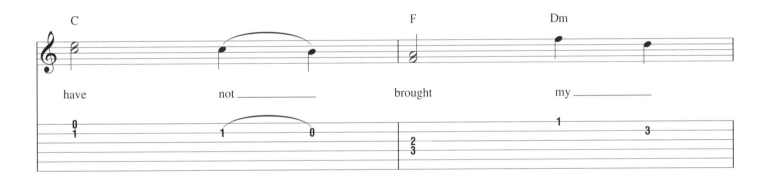

specs with me. 2. There were me.

Additional Lyrics

2. There were rats, rats,
   As big as bloomin' cats,
   In the store, in the store.
   There were rats, rats,
   As big as bloomin' cats,
   In the quartermaster's store.

3. There was bread, bread,
   Harder than your head,
   In the store, in the store.
   There was bread, bread,
   Harder than your head,
   In the quartermaster's store.

Ride a Cock Horse

Traditional

Rock-a-Bye, Baby

Traditional

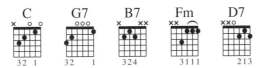

Strum Pattern: 7
Pick Pattern: 8
Moderately

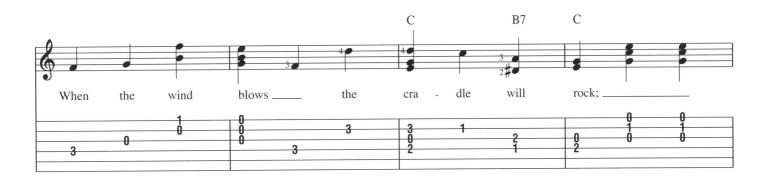

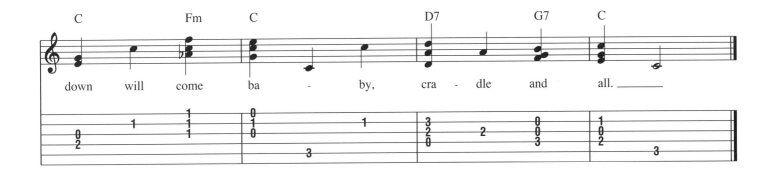

Ring Around the Rosie

Traditional

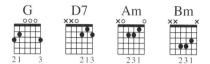

Strum Pattern: 8
Pick Pattern: 8

Brightly, in 2

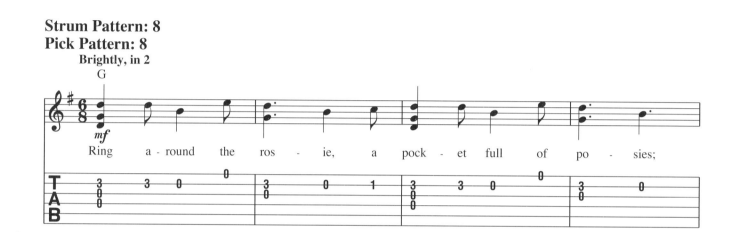

Ring a-round the ros - ie, a pock - et full of po - sies;

ash - es, ash - es, we all fall down. _____

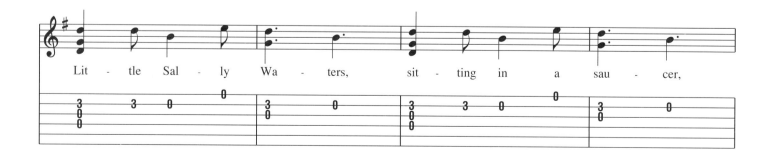

Lit - tle Sal - ly Wa - ters, sit - ting in a sau - cer,

weep - ing and a - moan - ing like a tur - tle dove. _____

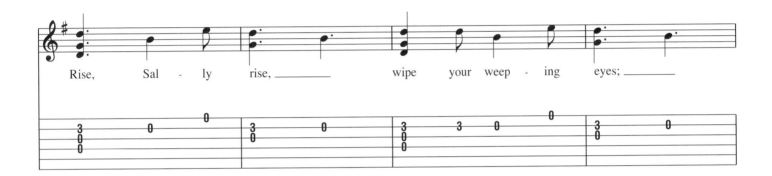

Rise, Sal - ly rise, _____ wipe your weep - ing eyes; _____

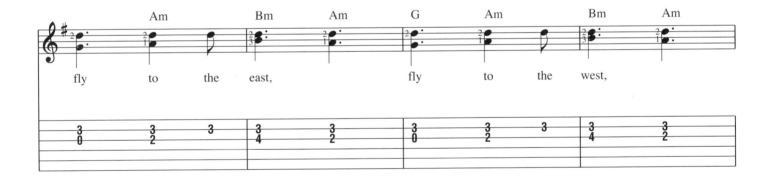

fly to the east, fly to the west,

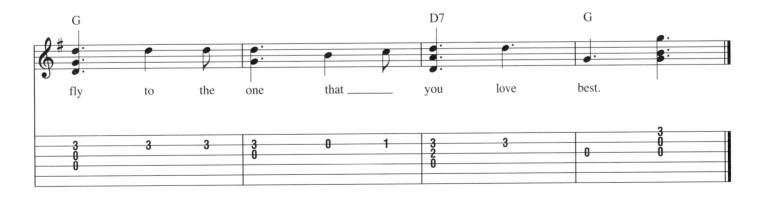

fly to the one that _____ you love best.

Round and Round the Garden

Traditional

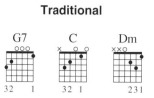

Strum Pattern: 8
Pick Pattern: 8

Intro
Moderately, in 2

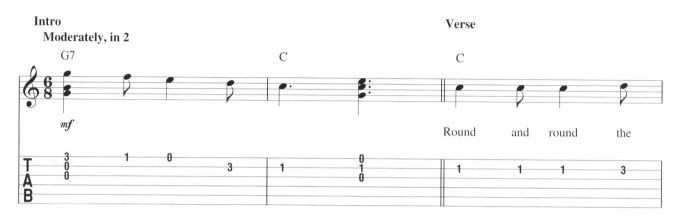

Round and round the

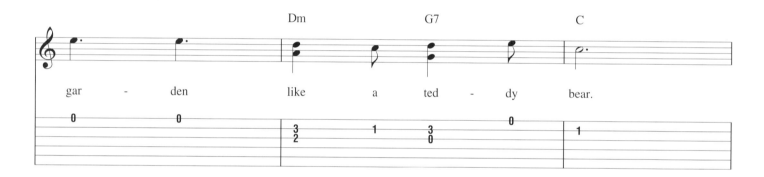

gar - den like a ted - dy bear.

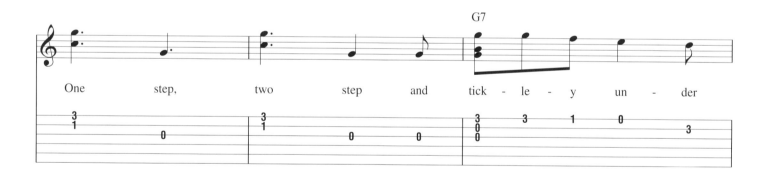

One step, two step and tick - le - y un - der

there!

Round the Village

Traditional

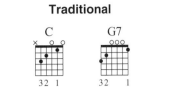

Strum Pattern: 3
Pick Pattern: 3

Verse

Moderately

1. Go round and round the vil - lage, go round and round the
2. - 5. *See additional lyrics*

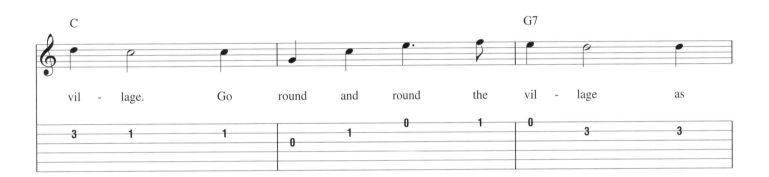

vil - lage. Go round and round the vil - lage as

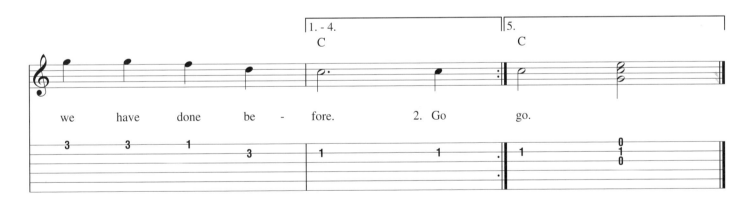

we have done be - fore. 2. Go go.

Additional Lyrics

2. Go in and out the windows,
   Go in and out the windows.
   Go in and out the windows
   As we have done before.

3. Now stand and face your partner,
   Now stand and face your partner.
   Now stand and face your partner
   And bow before you go.

4. Now follow me to London,
   Now follow me to London.
   Now follow me to London
   As we have done before.

5. Now shake his hand and leave him,
   Now shake his hand and leave him.
   Now shake his hand and leave him
   And bow before you go.

Row, Row, Row Your Boat

Traditional

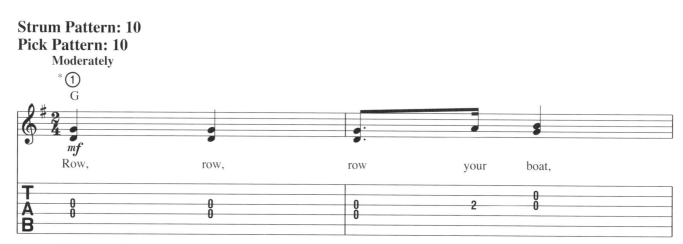

Strum Pattern: 10
Pick Pattern: 10
Moderately

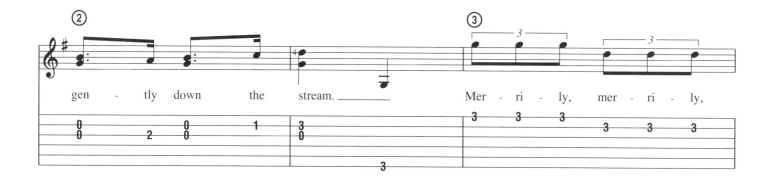

*This song can be sung as a 4-part round.

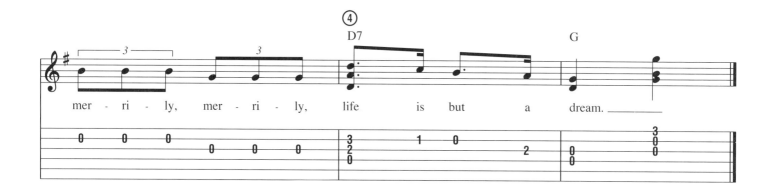

Rub-a-Dub-Dub,
Three Men in a Tub

Traditional

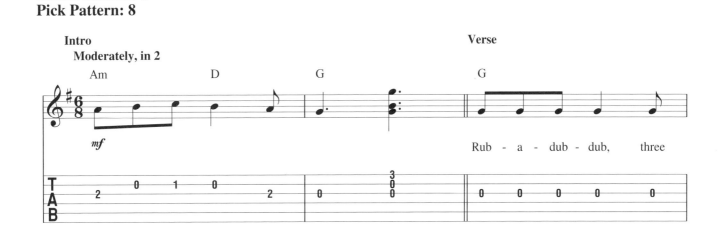

Strum Pattern: 8
Pick Pattern: 8

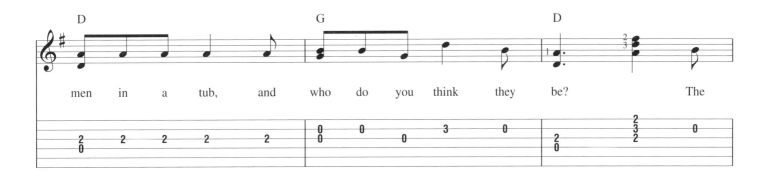

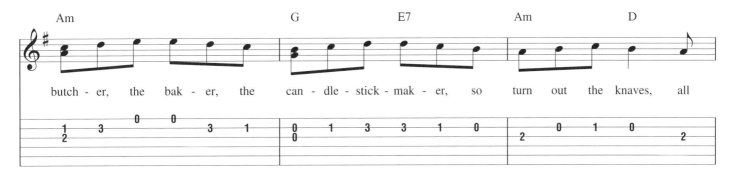

See Saw, Margery Daw

Traditional

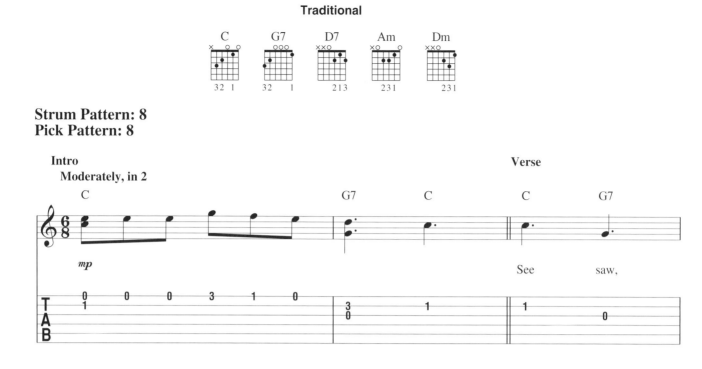

Strum Pattern: 8
Pick Pattern: 8

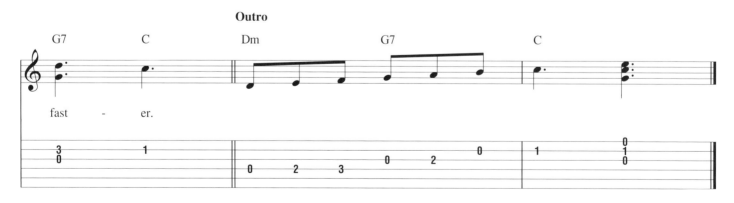

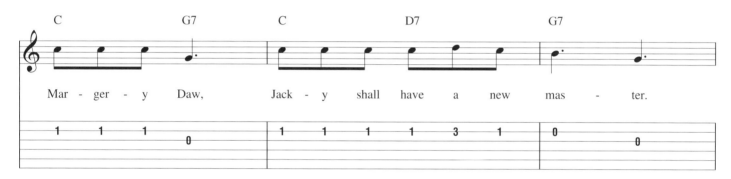

She'll Be Comin' 'Round the Mountain

Traditional

Strum Pattern: 2
Pick Pattern: 4

Additional Lyrics

2. She'll be drivin' six white horses when she comes.
She'll be drivin' six white horses when she comes.
She'll be drivin' six white horses,
She'll be drivin' six white horses,
She'll be drivin' six white horses when she comes.

3. Oh, we'll all go out to meet her when she comes.
Oh, we'll all go out to meet her when she comes.
Oh, we'll all go out to meet her,
Oh, we'll all go out to meet her,
Yes, we'll all go out to meet her when she comes.

4. She'll be wearin' a blue bonnet when she comes.
She'll be wearin' a blue bonnet when she comes.
She'll be wearin' a blue bonnet,
She'll be wearin' a blue bonnet,
She'll be wearin' a blue bonnet when she comes.

Short'nin' Bread

Plantation Song

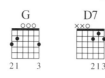

Strum Pattern: 3
Pick Pattern: 3

Verse
Moderately, in 2

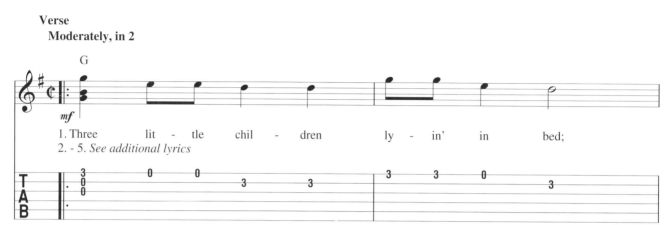

1. Three lit - tle chil - dren ly - in' in bed;
2. - 5. *See additional lyrics*

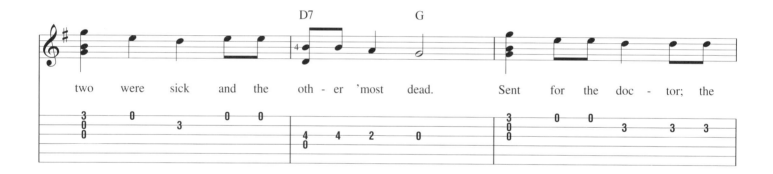

two were sick and the oth - er 'most dead. Sent for the doc - tor; the

doc - tor said, "Feed those chil - dren on short - 'nin' bread."

Chorus

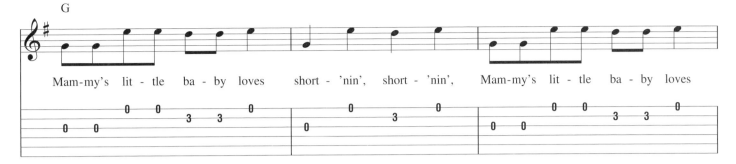

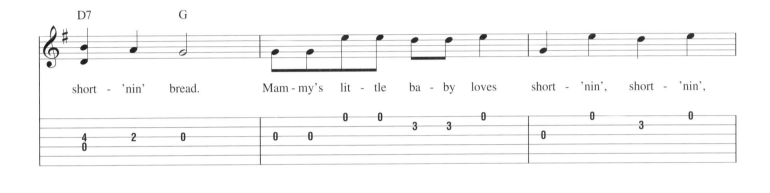

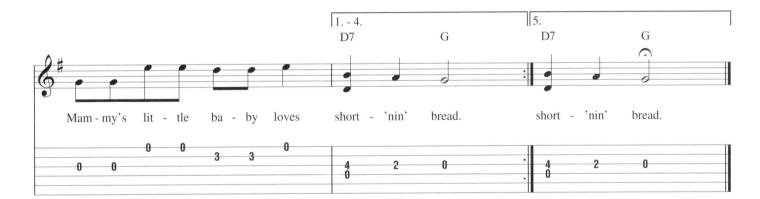

Additional Lyrics

2. Put in the skillet, put on the lid,
   Mammy's gonna bake a little short'nin' bread.
   That ain't all she's gonna do,
   Mammy's gonna make a little coffee too.

3. Then the little child, sick in bed,
   When he hear tell of short'nin' bread,
   Popped up well, he dance an' sing,
   He almos' cut the pigeon wing.

4. I slip to the kitchen, slip up the lid,
   Filled mah pockets full of short'nin' bread,
   Stole the skillet, stole the lid,
   Stole the gal makin' short'nin' bread.

5. They caught me with the skillet, they caught me with the lid,
   They caught me with the gal makin' short'nin' bread,
   Paid for the skillet, paid for the lid,
   Spent six months in jail eatin' short'nin' bread.

Simple Simon

Traditional

Strum Pattern: 10
Pick Pattern: 10

Moderately

Sim - ple Si - mon met a pie - man go - ing to the fair. ___ Said

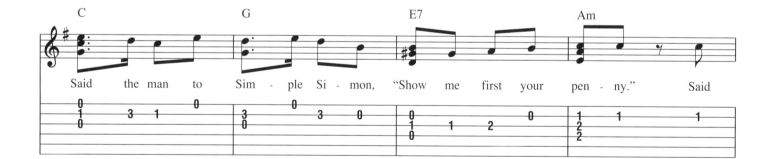

Sim - ple Si - mon to the pie - man, "Let me taste your ware." ___

Said the man to Sim - ple Si - mon, "Show me first your pen - ny." Said

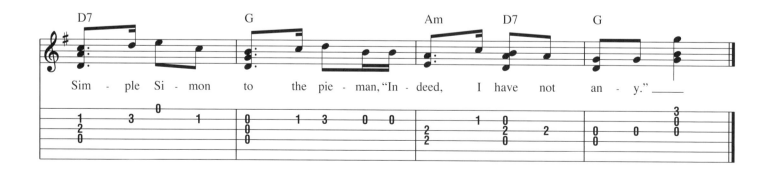

Sim - ple Si - mon to the pie - man, "In - deed, I have not an - y." ___

Skip to My Lou

Traditional

Strum Pattern: 10
Pick Pattern: 10

Additional Lyrics

2. Lost my partner, what'll I do?
   Lost my partner, what'll I do?
   Lost my partner, what'll I do?
   Skip to my lou, my darlin'.

3. I'll get another one purtier than you,
   I'll get another one purtier than you,
   I'll get another one purtier than you,
   Skip to my lou, my darlin'.

4. Can't get a red bird, a blue bird'll do,
   Can't get a red bird, a blue bird'll do,
   Can't get a red bird, a blue bird'll do,
   Skip to my lou, my darlin'.

Sing a Song of Sixpence

Traditional

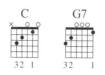

Strum Pattern: 8
Pick Pattern: 8

Verse
Moderately, in 2

1. Sing a song of six - pence, a pock - et full of
2. *See additional lyrics*

rye; _____ four and twen - ty black - birds baked in a pie. _____ When the pie was

baked in a pie. _____ When the pie was

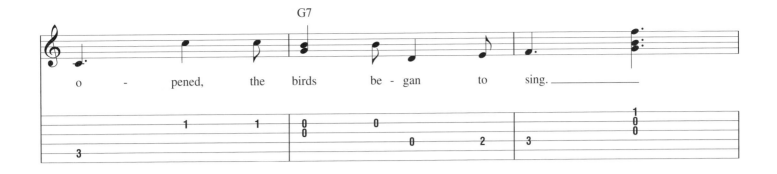

o - pened, the birds be - gan to sing.

Was - n't that a dain - ty dish to

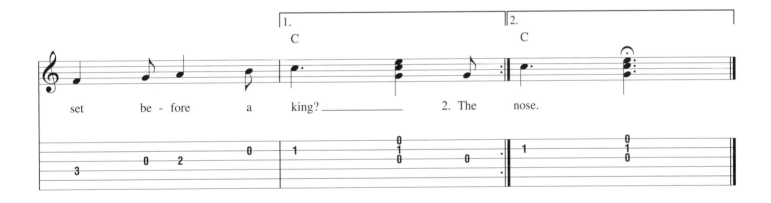

set be - fore a king? 2. The nose.

Additional Lyrics

2. The king was in the counting house,
   Counting all his money.
   The queen was in the parlor,
   Eating bread and honey.
   The maid was in the garden,
   Hanging out the clothes.
   Along came a blackbird
   And pecked off her nose.

Sleep, Baby, Sleep

Pennsylvania Dutch Lullaby

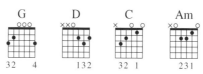

Strum Pattern: 8
Pick Pattern: 8

Verse
Moderately, in 2

1. Sleep, ba - by, sleep. Your dad - dy's tend - ing the sheep. Your
2., 3. *See additional lyrics*

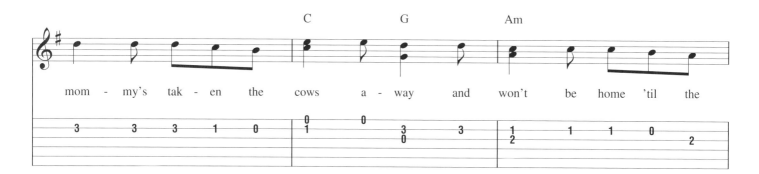

mom - my's tak - en the cows a - way and won't be home 'til the

break of day. Sleep, ba - by, sleep. sleep.

Additional Lyrics

2. Sleep, baby, sleep.
Your daddy's tending the sheep.
Your mommy's tending the little ones;
Baby sleep as long as he wants.
Sleep, baby, sleep.

3. Sleep, baby, sleep.
Your daddy's tending the sheep.
Your mommy's off too in gossiping flight
And won't be back 'til late tonight.
Sleep, baby, sleep.

Sur le Pont d'Avignon

French Folksong

Strum Pattern: 3
Pick Pattern: 3

Verse
Fast

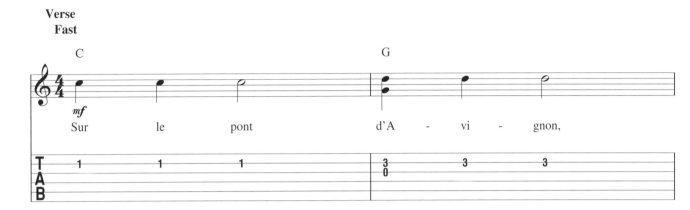

Sur le pont d'A - vi - gnon,

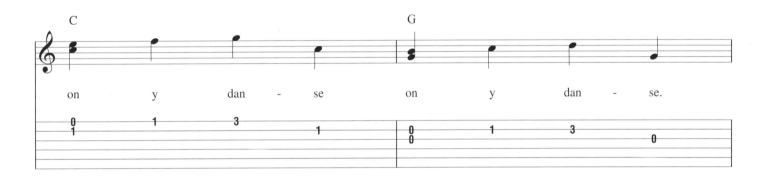

on y dan - se on y dan - se.

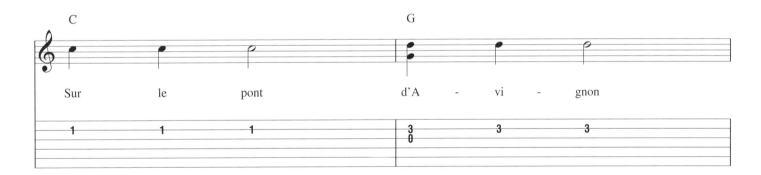

Sur le pont d'A - vi - gnon

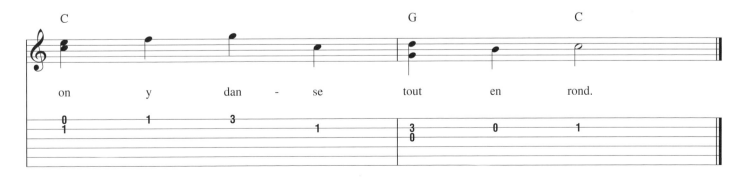

on y dan - se tout en rond.

Soldier, Soldier Will You Marry Me

Folk Song

Strum Pattern: 3
Pick Pattern: 3

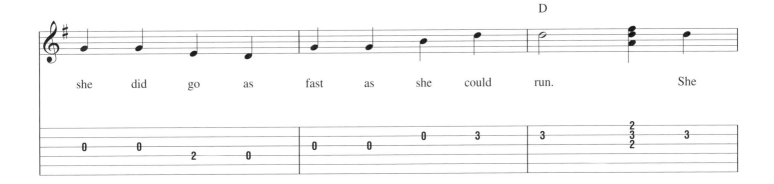

she did go as fast as she could run. She

brought him back the fin - est that was there, and the sol - dier put them

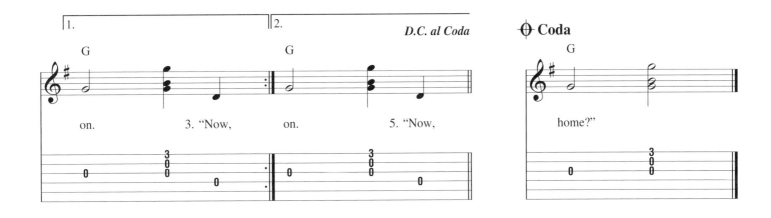

on.   3. "Now,   on.   5. "Now,   home?"

Additional Lyrics

3. "Now, soldier, soldier, will you marry me
   With your musket, fife and drum?"
   "Oh, how can I marry such a pretty little girl
   When I have no coat to put on?"

4. Then off to the tailor she did go
   As fast as she could run.
   She brought him back the finest that was there,
   And the soldier put it on.

5. "Now, soldier, soldier, will you marry me
   With your musket, fife and drum?"
   "Oh, how can I marry such a pretty little girl
   When I've a good wife and baby at home?"

Teddy Bear

Rope-Jumping Chant

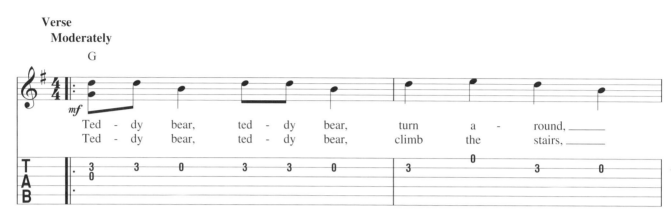

Strum Pattern: 3
Pick Pattern: 3

Verse
Moderately

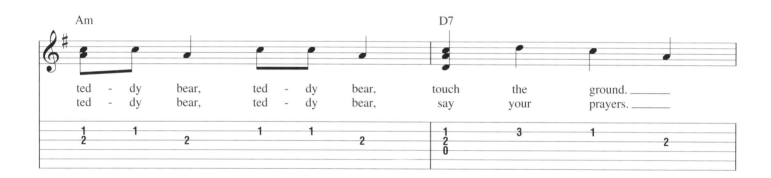

Ted - dy bear, ted - dy bear, turn a - round, _____
Ted - dy bear, ted - dy bear, climb the stairs, _____

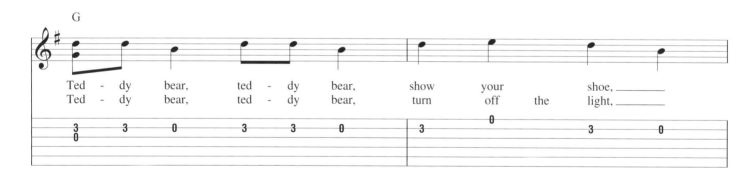

ted - dy bear, ted - dy bear, touch the ground. _____
ted - dy bear, ted - dy bear, say your prayers. _____

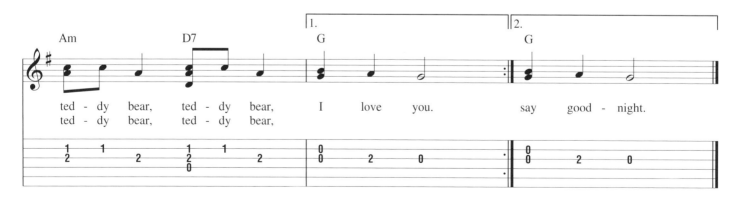

Ted - dy bear, ted - dy bear, show your shoe, _____
Ted - dy bear, ted - dy bear, turn off the light, _____

ted - dy bear, ted - dy bear, I love you. say good - night.
ted - dy bear, ted - dy bear,

Ten Green Bottles

Traditional

Strum Pattern: 3
Pick Pattern: 3

Additional Lyrics

2. Nine green bottles hanging on the wall.*(Repeat)*
   And if one green bottle should accident'ly fall
   There'll be eight green bottles hanging on the wall.

3. Eight green bottles hanging on the wall.*(Repeat)*
   And if one green bottle should accident'ly fall
   There'll be seven green bottles hanging on the wall.

4. Seven green bottles hanging on the wall.*(Repeat)*
   And if one green bottle should accident'ly fall
   There'll be six green bottles hanging on the wall.

5. Six green bottles hanging on the wall.*(Repeat)*
   And if one green bottle should accident'ly fall
   There'll be five green bottles hanging on the wall.

6. Five green bottles hanging on the wall.*(Repeat)*
   And if one green bottle should accident'ly fall
   There'll be four green bottles hanging on the wall.

7. Four green bottles hanging on the wall.*(Repeat)*
   And if one green bottle should accident'ly fall
   There'll be three green bottles hanging on the wall.

8. Three green bottles hanging on the wall.*(Repeat)*
   And if one green bottle should accident'ly fall
   There'll be two green bottles hanging on the wall.

9. Two green bottles hanging on the wall.*(Repeat)*
   And if one green bottle should accident'ly fall
   There'll be one green bottle hanging on the wall.

10. One green bottles hanging on the wall.*(Repeat)*
    And if that green bottle should accident'ly fall
    There'll be no green bottles hanging on the wall.

Ten Little Indians

Traditional

Strum Pattern: 3
Pick Pattern: 3

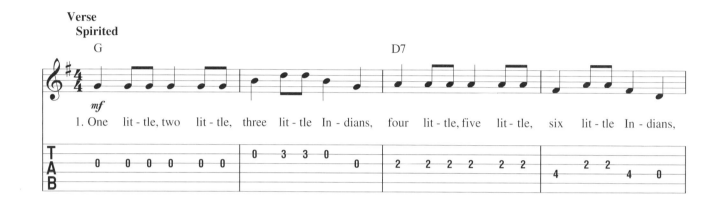

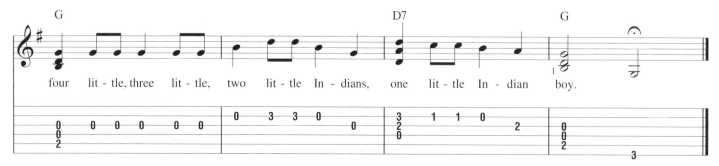

Ten Little Pigs

Traditional

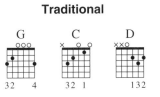

Strum Pattern: 3
Pick Pattern: 3

Verse
Moderately

1. Ten lit - tle pigs went to mar - ket. One of them ___ fell
2. - 5. *See additional lyrics*

down. One of them, ___ he ran a - way. ___

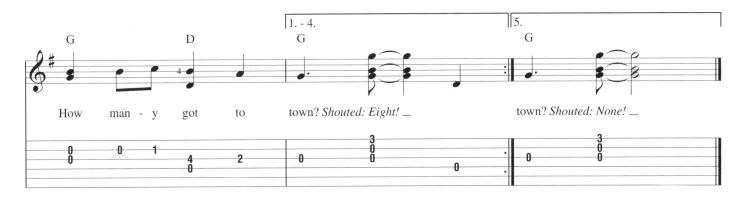

How man - y got to town? *Shouted: Eight!* ___ town? *Shouted: None!* ___

Additional Lyrics

2. Eight little pigs went to market.
One of them fell down.
One of them, he ran away.
How many got to town?
Shouted: Six!

3. Six little pigs went to market.
One of them fell down.
One of them, he ran away.
How many got to town?
Shouted: Four!

4. Four little pigs went to market.
One of them fell down.
One of them, he ran away.
How many got to town?
Shouted: Two!

5. Two little pigs went to market.
One of them fell down.
One of them, he ran away.
How many got to town?
Shouted: None!

There Was a Crooked Man

Traditional

Strum Pattern: 10
Pick Pattern: 10

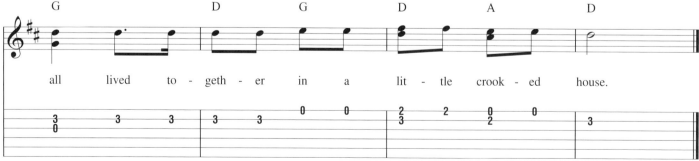

There Was a Princess

Traditional

Strum Pattern: 3
Pick Pattern: 3

Additional Lyrics

2. And she lived in a big high tower,
   Big high tower, big high tower.
   And she lived in a big high tower,
   Big high tower.

3. One day a bad queen cast a spell,
   Cast a spell, cast a spell.
   One day a bad queen cast a spell,
   Cast a spell.

4. The princess slept for a hundred years,
   A hundred years, a hundred years.
   The princess slept for a hundred years,
   A hundred years.

5. A great big forest grew around,
   Grew around, grew around.
   A great big forest grew around,
   Grew around.

6. A gallant prince came riding by,
   Riding by, riding by.
   A gallant prince came riding by,
   Riding by.

7. He cut the trees down with his sword,
   With his sword, with his sword.
   He cut the trees down with his sword,
   With his sword.

8. He woke the princess with a kiss,
   With a kiss, with a kiss.
   He woke the princess with a kiss,
   With a kiss.

9. So everybody's happy now,
   Happy now, happy now.
   So everybody's happy now,
   Happy now.

There Was an Old Frog

Traditional

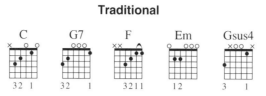

Strum Pattern: 3
Pick Pattern: 3

Verse

Fast

1. There was an old frog and he lived in the spring,
2. - 4. *See additional lyrics*

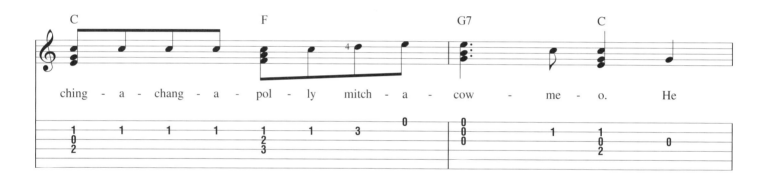

ching - a - chang - a - pol - ly mitch - a - cow - me - o. He

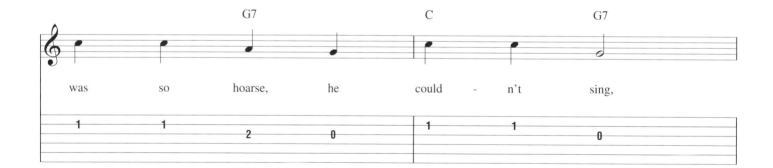

was so hoarse, he could - n't sing,

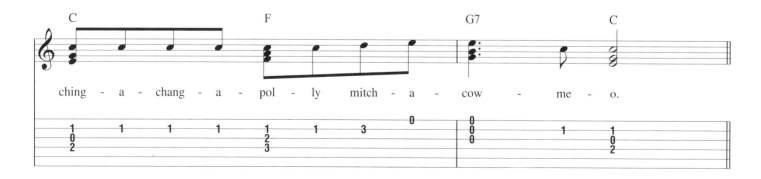

ching - a - chang - a - pol - ly mitch - a - cow - me - o.

Chorus

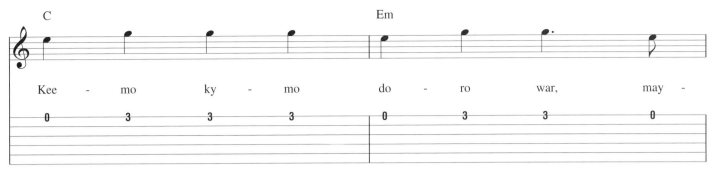

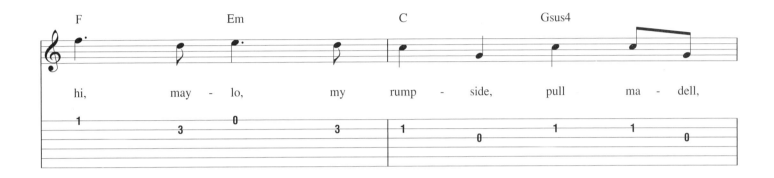

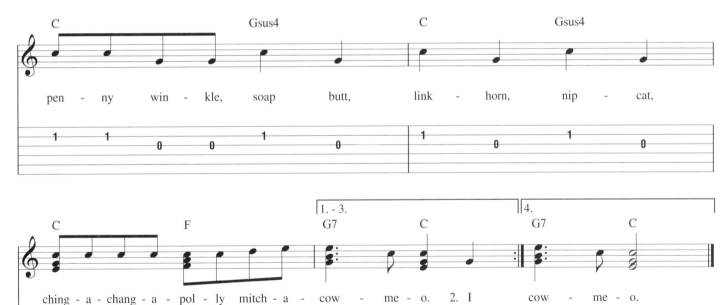

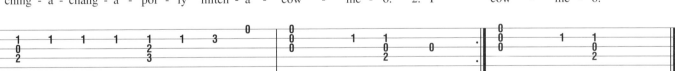

Additional Lyrics

2. I grabbed him by the leg and pulled him out,
Ching-a-chang-a-polly mitch-a-cow-me-o.
He hopped and he skipped and he bounced all about,
Ching-a-chang-a-polly mitch-a-cow-me-o.

3. Cheese in the spring house nine days old,
Ching-a-chang-a-polly mitch-a-cow-me-o.
Rats and skippers is a getting mighty bold,
Ching-a-chang-a-polly mitch-a-cow-me-o.

4. Big fat rat and a bucket of souse,
Ching-a-chang-a-polly mitch-a-cow-me-o.
Take it back to the big white house,
Ching-a-chang-a-polly mitch-a-cow-me-o.

There Was an Old Man

Traditional

Strum Pattern: 3
Pick Pattern: 3

Verse
Moderately

1. There _ was an old _ man who _ lived _ in a wood, as _ you may plain - ly
2. - 7. *See additional lyrics*

see. He _ said he could do as much work in a day as his

wife _ could _ do in three. 2. "With _ will!"

Additional Lyrics

2. "With all my heart," the old woman said,
   "If that you will allow,
   Tomorrow you'll stay at home in my stead,
   And I'll go drive the plough."

3. "But you must milk the Tidy cow,
   For fear that she go dry;
   And you must feed the little pigs
   That are within the sty."

4. "And you must mind the speckled hen,
   For fear she lay away;
   And you must reel a spool of yarn
   That I spun yesterday."

5. The old woman took a staff in her hand
   And went to drive the plough;
   The old man took a pail in his hand
   And went to milk the cow.

6. But Tidy hinched and Tidy flinched
   And Tidy broke his nose;
   And Tidy gave him such a blow
   That blood ran down to his toes.

7. "Hi Tidy! Ho Tidy! High!
   Tidy do stand still!
   If ever I milk you, Tidy, again,
   'Twill be sore against my will!"

There Was an Old Woman Who Lived in a Shoe

Traditional

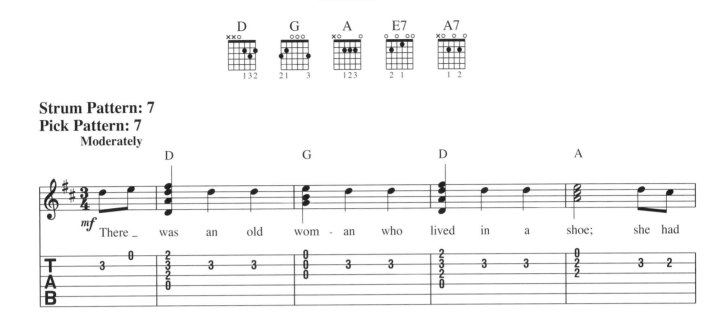

Strum Pattern: 7
Pick Pattern: 7

Moderately

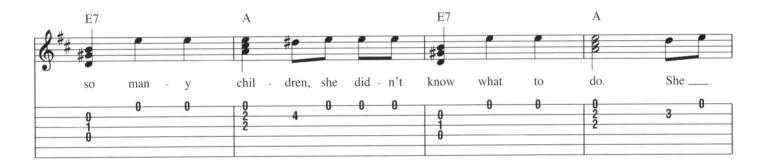

There _ was an old wom - an who lived in a shoe; she had

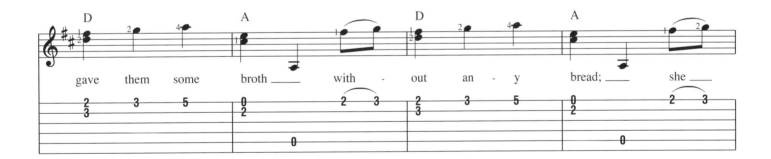

so man - y chil - dren, she did - n't know what to do. She ___

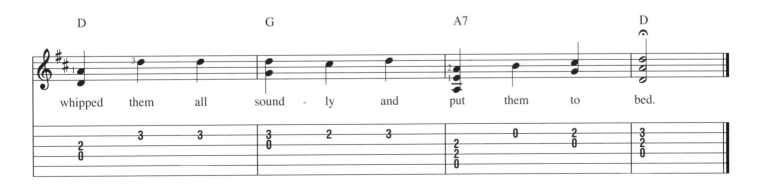

gave them some broth ___ with - out an - y bread; ___ she ___

whipped them all sound - ly and put them to bed.

There Were Ten in a Bed

Traditional

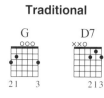

Strum Pattern: 10
Pick Pattern: 10

Verse

Moderately

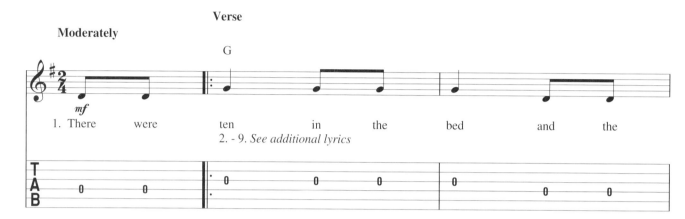

1. There were ten in the bed and the

2. - 9. See additional lyrics

lit - tle one said, "Roll o - ver,

roll o - ver!" So they

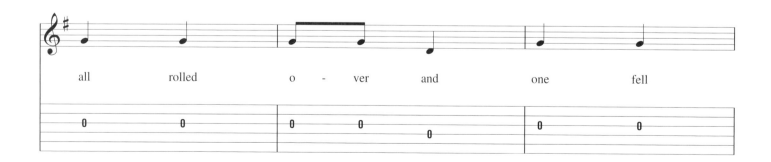

all rolled o - ver and one fell

Additional Lyrics

2. There were nine in the bed and the little one said,
   "Roll over, roll over!"
   So they all rolled over and one fell out.

3. There were eight in the bed and the little one said,
   "Roll over, roll over!"
   So they all rolled over and one fell out.

4. There were seven in the bed and the little one said,
   "Roll over, roll over!"
   So they all rolled over and one fell out.

5. There were six in the bed and the little one said,
   "Roll over, roll over!"
   So they all rolled over and one fell out.

6. There were five in the bed and the little one said,
   "Roll over, roll over!"
   So they all rolled over and one fell out.

7. There were four in the bed and the little one said,
   "Roll over, roll over!"
   So they all rolled over and one fell out.

8. There were three in the bed and the little one said,
   "Roll over, roll over!"
   So they all rolled over and one fell out.

9. There were two in the bed and the little one said,
   "Roll over, roll over!"
   So they all rolled over and one fell out.

There's a Hole in the Bucket

Traditional

Strum Pattern: 8
Pick Pattern: 8

Verse
Moderately

1. There's a hole in the buck – et, dear Li – za, dear Li – za. There's a
   fix it, dear Hen – ry, dear Hen – ry, dear Hen – ry. Well, __

3.–19. See additional lyrics

hole in the buck – et, dear Li – za, a hole! 2. Well, __ hole!
fix it, dear Hen – ry, dear Hen – ry, fix it! 3. With __

Additional Lyrics

3. With what shall I fix it, dear Liza, etc.
4. With a straw, dear Henry, etc.
5. But the straw is too long, dear Liza, etc.
6. Then cut it, dear Henry, etc.
7. With what shall I cut it, dear Liza, etc.
8. With a knife, dear Henry, etc.
9. But the knife is too dull, dear Liza, etc.
10. Then sharpen it, dear Henry, etc.
11. With what shall I sharpen it, dear Liza, etc.
12. With a stone, dear Henry, etc.
13. But the stone is too dry, dear Liza, etc.
14. Then wet it, dear Henry, etc.
15. With what shall I wet it, dear Liza, etc.
16. With water, dear Henry, etc.
17. In what shall I carry it, dear Liza, etc.
18. In a bucket, dear Henry, etc.
19. There's a hole in the bucket, dear Liza, etc.

This Little Pig Went to Market

Traditional

Strum Pattern: 3
Pick Pattern: 3

This Old Man

Traditional

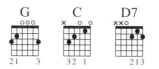

Strum Pattern: 4, 3
Pick Pattern: 3, 4

Verse
Lively

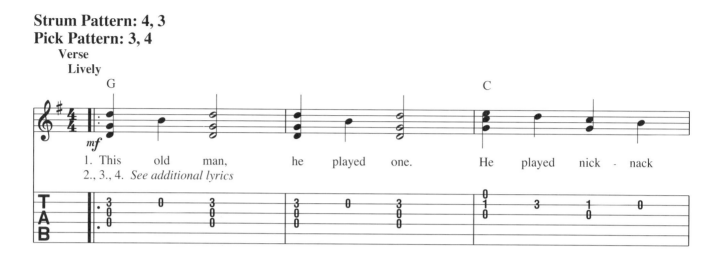

1. This old man, he played one. He played nick - nack
2., 3., 4. *See additional lyrics*

on my drum with a nick - nack pad - dy whack, give your dog a bone.

This old man came roll - ing home. _____ roll - ing home.

Additional Lyrics

2. This old man, he played two.
   He played nicknack on my shoe with a
   Nicknack paddy whack, give your dog a bone.
   This old man came rolling home.

3. This old man, he played three.
   He played nicknack on my knee with a
   Nicknack paddy whack, give your dog a bone.
   This old man came rolling home.

4. This old man, he played four.
   He played nicknack on my door with a
   Nicknack paddy whack, give your dog a bone.
   This old man came rolling home.

Three Blind Mice

Traditional

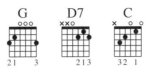

Strum Pattern: 8
Pick Pattern: 8

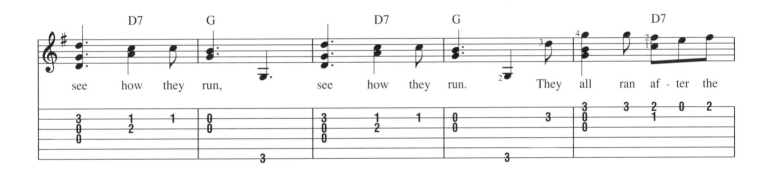

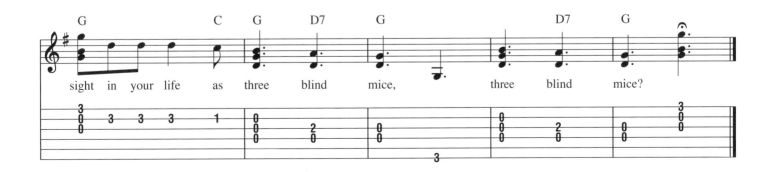

Three Little Kittens

Traditional

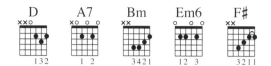

D   A7   Bm   Em6   F#

Strum Pattern: 8
Pick Pattern: 8

Verse
Moderately, in 2

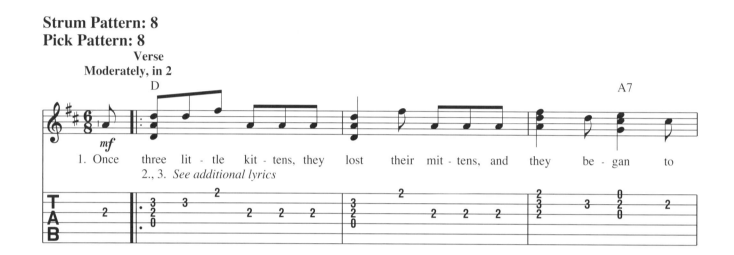

1. Once three lit - tle kit - tens, they lost their mit - tens, and they be - gan to
2., 3. *See additional lyrics*

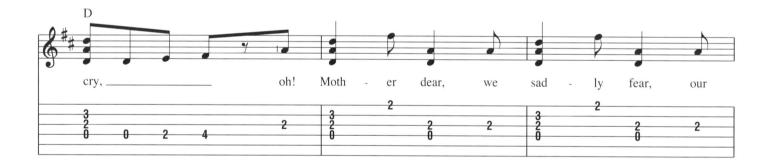

cry, _____ oh! Moth - er dear, we sad - ly fear, our

mit - tens we have lost. _____ What, lost your mit - tens, you

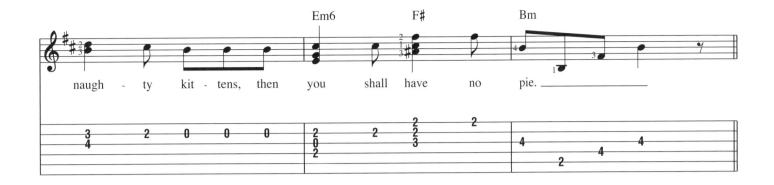

naugh - ty kit - tens, then you shall have no pie. _____

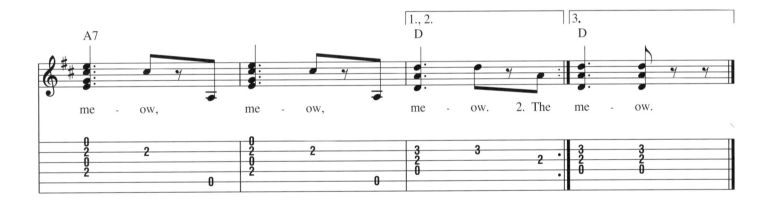

Chorus

Me - ow, me - ow, me - ow, me - ow,

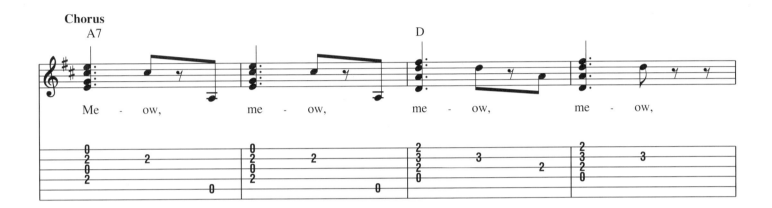

me - ow, me - ow, me - ow. 2. The me - ow.

Additional Lyrics

2. The three little kittens
   They found their mittens,
   And they began to cry,
   Oh! Mother dear, see here, see here,
   Our mittens we have found.
   What, found your mittens, you darling kittens,
   Then you shall have some pie.

3. The three little kittens
   Put on their mittens,
   And soon ate up the pie,
   Oh! Mother dear, we greatly fear,
   Our mittens we have soil'd.
   What, soil'd your mittens, you naughty kittens,
   Then they began to cry.

Tom, Tom, the Piper's Son

Traditional

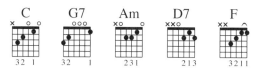

Strum Pattern: 10
Pick Pattern: 10

Verse
Moderately

Tom, Tom, the Pi-per's son, stole a pig and a-way he run! The

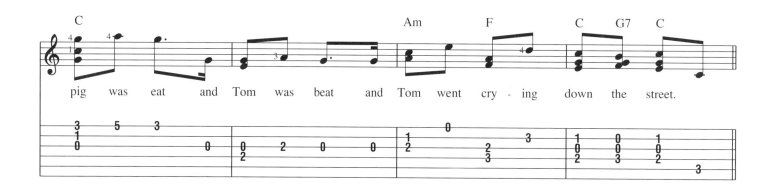

pig was eat and Tom was beat and Tom went cry-ing down the street.

Outro

Tommy Thumb

Traditional

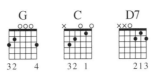

Strum Pattern: 10
Pick Pattern: 10

Verse
Moderately fast

1. Tom - my Thumb, Tom - my Thumb, where are
2. - 6. *See additional lyrics*

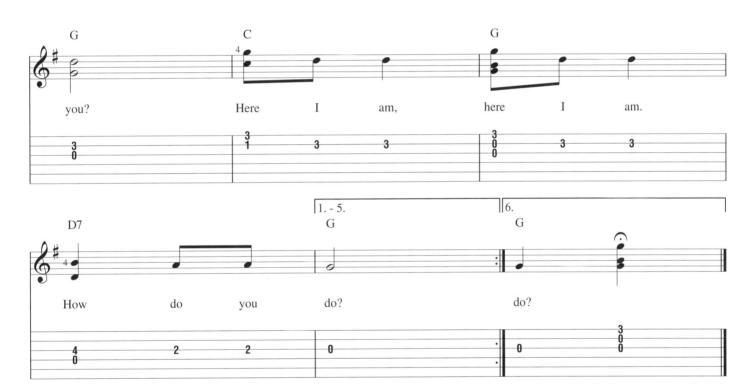

you? Here I am, here I am.

How do you do? do?

Additional Lyrics

2. Peter Pointer, Peter Pointer,
   Where are you?
   Here I am, here I am.
   How do you do?

3. Middle Man, Middle Man,
   Where are you?
   Here I am, here I am.
   How do you do?

4. Ruby Ring, Ruby Ring,
   Where are you?
   Here I am, here I am.
   How do you do?

5. Baby Small, Baby Small,
   Where are you?
   Here I am, here I am.
   How do you do?

6. Fingers all, fingers all,
   Where are you?
   Here we are, here we are.
   How do you do?

Turn Again Whittington

Traditional

Strum Pattern: 7
Pick Pattern: 7

Twinkle, Twinkle Little Star

Traditional

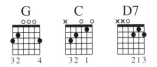

Strum Pattern: 3
Pick Pattern: 3, 4

Moderately

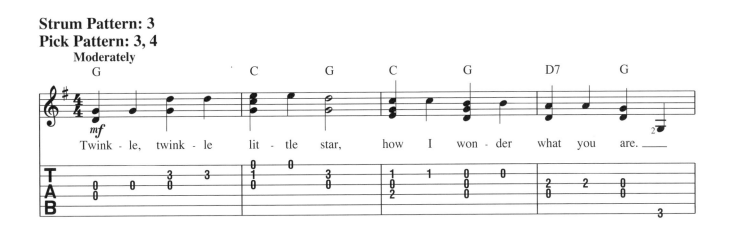

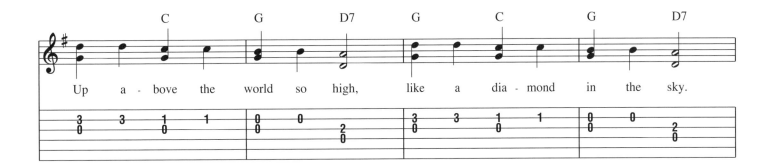

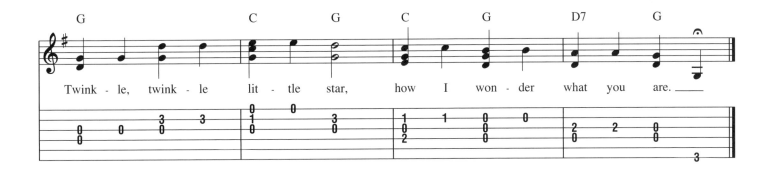

Two Little Chickens

Traditional

Strum Pattern: 3
Pick Pattern: 3

Verse
Moderately

1. Two lit - tle chick-ens look-ing for some more, a - long came an-oth - er two and
2. - 4. *See additional lyrics*

they make four. Run to the hay - stack, run to the pen,

run lit - tle chick - ens, back to Moth - er Hen. back to Moth - er Hen.

Additional Lyrics

2. Four little chickens getting in a fix,
   Along came another two and they make six.

3. Six little chickens perching on a gate,
   Along came another two and they make eight.

4. Eight little chickens run to Mother Hen,
   Along came another two and they make ten.

Two Little Dickie Birds

Traditional

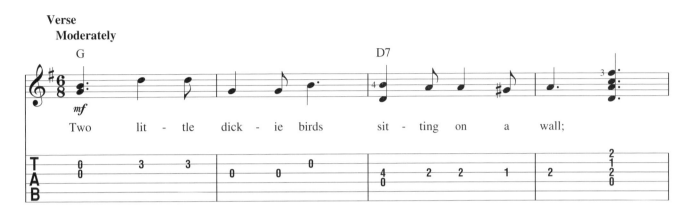

Strum Pattern: 8
Pick Pattern: 8

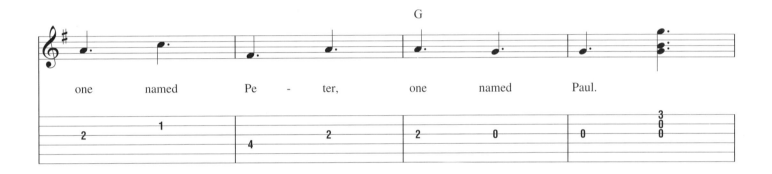

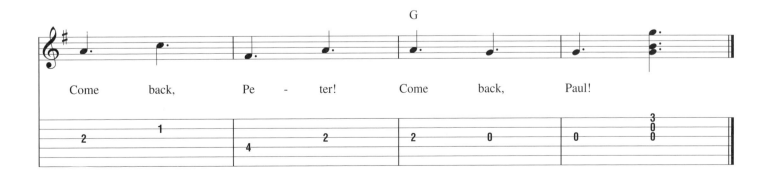

Underneath the Spreading Chestnut Tree

Traditional

Strum Pattern: 10
Pick Pattern: 10

1., 2. Un - der - neath the spread - ing _____ chest - nut tree,

I'm as hap - py as can be

with my ban - jo on my knee

un - der - neath the spread - ing _____ chest - nut tree. tree.

Wee Willie Winkie

Traditional

Strum Pattern: 3
Pick Pattern: 3

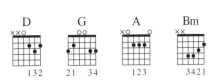

Verse
Moderately

1., 2. Wee Wil - lie Wink - ie runs through the town, up - stairs and down - stairs

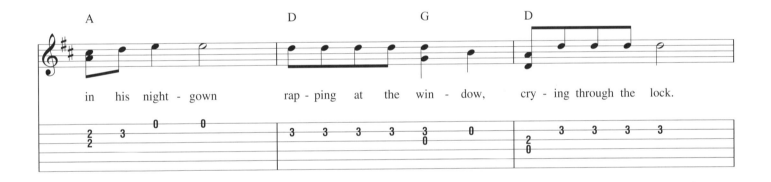

in his night - gown rap - ping at the win - dow, cry - ing through the lock.

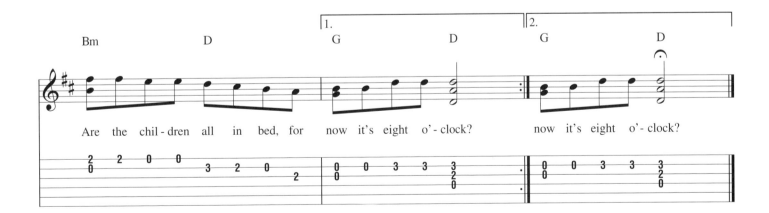

Are the chil - dren all in bed, for now it's eight o' - clock? now it's eight o' - clock?

What Are Little Boys Made Of?

Traditional

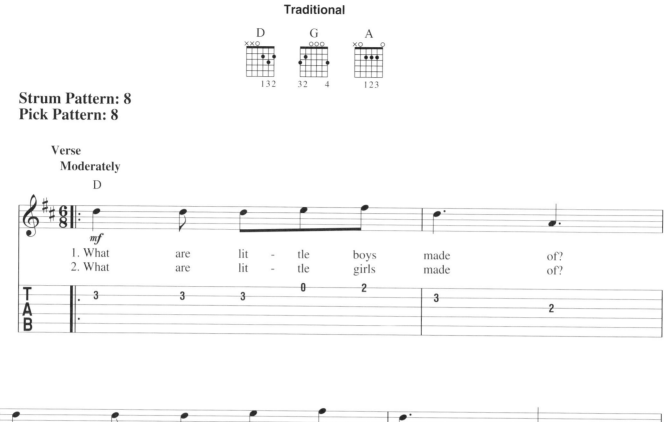

Strum Pattern: 8
Pick Pattern: 8

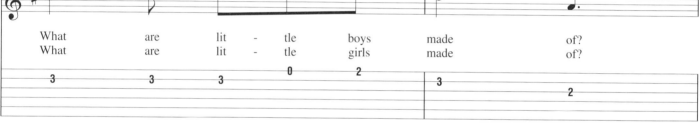

Verse
Moderately

1. What are lit - tle boys made of?
2. What are lit - tle girls made of?

What are lit - tle boys made of?
What are lit - tle girls made of?

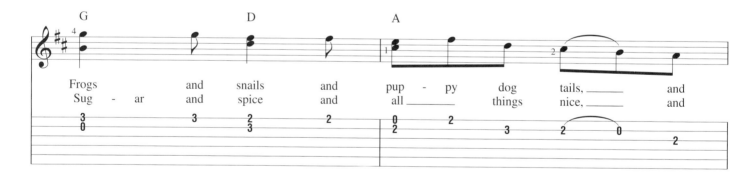

Frogs and snails and pup - py dog tails,_____ and
Sug - ar and spice and all_____ things nice,_____ and

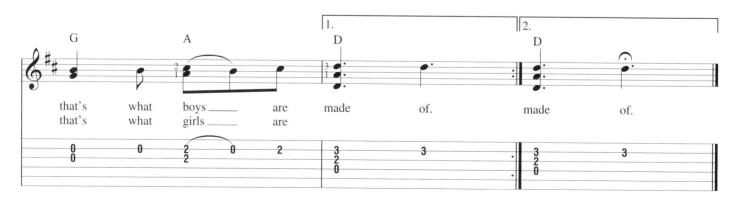

that's what boys_____ are made of.   made of.
that's what girls_____ are

The Wheels on the Bus

Traditional

Strum Pattern: 10
Pick Pattern: 10

Verse
Moderately

1. The wheels on the bus go round and round, round and
2. - 9. *See additional lyrics*

round, round and round. The wheels on the bus go round and

round all through the town. 2. The

Additional Lyrics

2. The wipers on the bus go swish, swish, swish,
Swish, swish, swish, swish, swish swish.
The wipers on the bus go swish, swish, swish
All through the town.

3. The horn on the bus goes beep, beep, beep,
Beep, beep, beep, beep, beep, beep.
The horn on the bus goes beep, beep, beep
All through the town.

4. The door on the bus goes open and shut,
Open and shut, open and shut.
The door on the bus goes open and shut
All through the town.

5. The people on the bus go up and down,
Up and down, up and down.
The people on the bus go up and down
All through the town.

6. The money on the bus goes clink, clink, clink,
Clink, clink, clink, clink, clink, clink.
The money on the bus goes clink, clink, clink
All through the town.

7. The driver on the bus says, "Move on back,
Move on back, move on back."
The driver on the bus says, "Move on back,"
All through the town.

8. The baby on the bus says, "Wah, wah, wah,
Wah, wah, wah, wah, wah, wah."
The baby on the bus says, "Wah, wah, wah,"
All through the town.

9. The mommy on the bus says, "Shh, shh, shh,
Shh, shh, shh, shh, shh, shh."
The mommy on the bus says, "Shh, shh, shh,"
All through the town.

When Johnny Comes Marching Home

Words and Music by Patrick Sarsfield Gilmore

Strum Pattern: 8
Pick Pattern: 8

Moderately, in 2

When John - ny comes march - ing home a - gain, hur - rah! _____ Hur - rah! _____ We'll

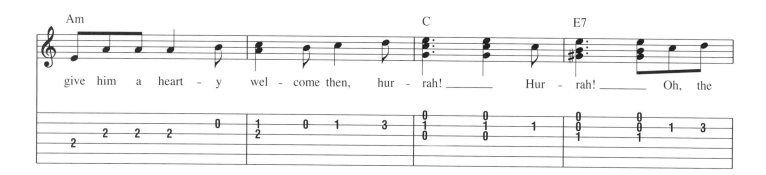

give him a heart - y wel - come then, hur - rah! _____ Hur - rah! _____ Oh, the

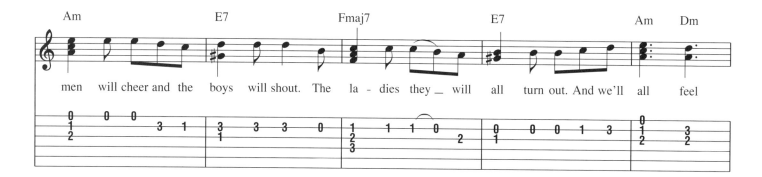

men will cheer and the boys will shout. The la - dies they _ will all turn out. And we'll all feel

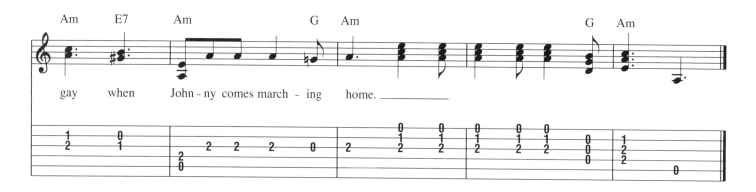

gay when John - ny comes march - ing home. _____

Where Are You Going to My Pretty Maid?

Traditional

Strum Pattern: 8
Pick Pattern: 8

Where Is Thumbkin?

Traditional

Strum Pattern: 3
Pick Pattern: 3

Additional Lyrics

2. Where is Pointer? Where is Pointer?
Here I am. Here I am.
How are you today, sir? Very well, I thank you.
Run away. Run away.

3. Where is Middle-man? Where is Middle-man?
Here I am. Here I am.
How are you today, sir? Very well, I thank you.
Run away. Run away.

4. Where is Ring-man? Where is Ring-man?
Here I am. Here I am.
How are you today, sir? Very well, I thank you.
Run away. Run away.

5. Where is Little-man? Where is Little-man?
Here I am. Here I am.
How are you today, sir? Very well, I thank you.
Run away. Run away.

Why Doesn't My Goose?

Traditional

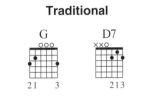

Strum Pattern: 3
Pick Pattern: 3

Verse
Moderately, in 2

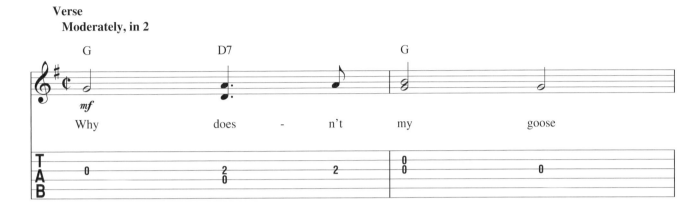

Why   does - n't   my   goose

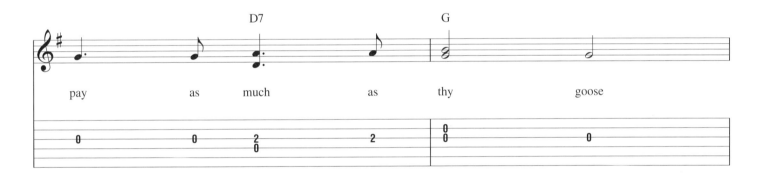

pay   as   much   as   thy   goose

when   I   paid   for   my   goose

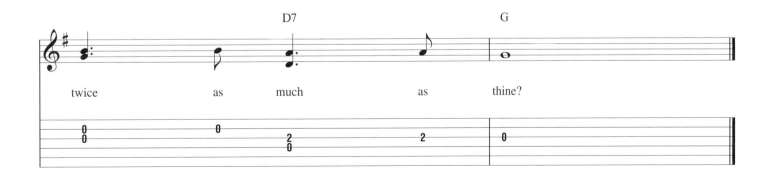

twice   as   much   as   thine?

Who Killed Cock Robin?

Traditional

Strum Pattern: 3
Pick Pattern: 3

Verse
Moderately

1. Who killed Cock Rob - in? "I," said the
2. - 13. *See additional lyrics*

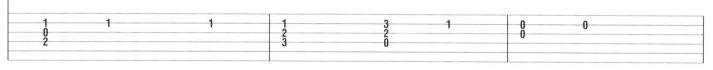

spar - row, "with my bow and ar - row,

I killed Cock Rob - in." All the birds of the air fell a

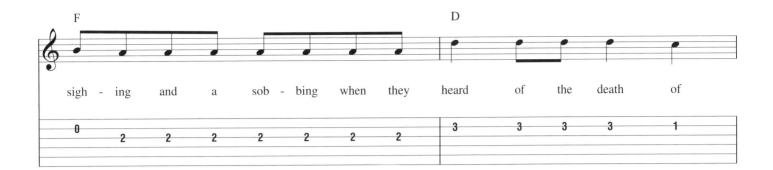

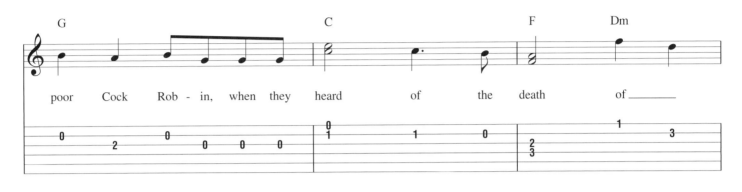

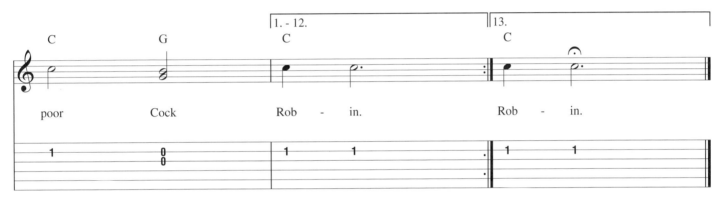

Additional Lyrics

2. Who saw him die?
"I," said the fly,
"With my little eye,
I saw him die."

3. Who caught his blood?
"I," said the fish,
"With my little dish,
I caught his blood."

4. Who'll make the shroud?
"I," said the beetle,
"With my thread and needle,
I'll make the shroud."

5. Who'll dig his grave?
"I," said the owl,
"With my pick and shovel,
I'll dig his grave."

6. Who'll be the parson?
"I," said the rook,
"With my little book,
I'll be the parson."

7. Who'll be the clerk?
"I," said the lark,
If it's not in the dark,
I'll be the clerk."

8. Who'll carry the link?
"I," said the linnet,
"I'll fetch it in a minute,
I'll carry the link."

9. Who'll be the chief mourner?
"I," said the dove,
"I mourn for my love,
I'll be chief mourner."

10. Who'll carry the coffin?
"I," said the kite,
"If it's not through the night,
I'll carry the coffin."

11. Who'll bear the pall?
"We," said the wren,
"Both the cock and the hen,
We'll bear the pall."

12. Who'll sing a psalm?
"I," said the thrush
As she sat on a bush,
"I'll sing a psalm."

13. Who'll toll the bell?
"I," said the bull,
"Because I can pull,
I'll toll the bell."

You'll Never Get to Heaven

Traditional

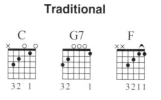

Strum Pattern: 3
Pick Pattern: 3

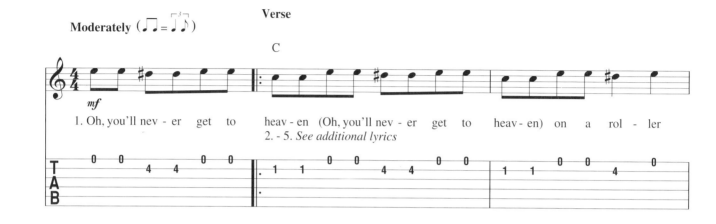

Chorus

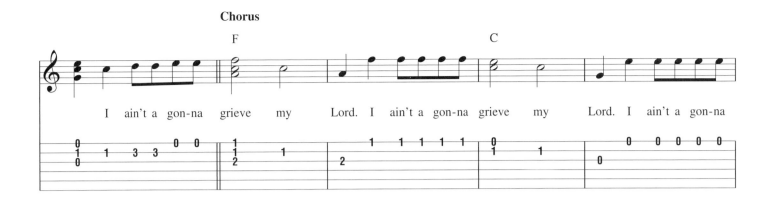

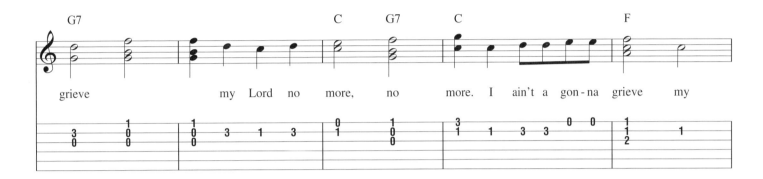

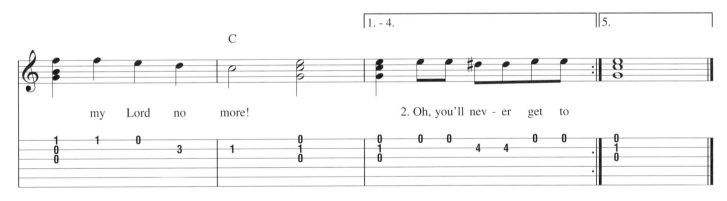

Additional Lyrics

2. Oh, you'll never get to heaven (Oh, you'll never get to heaven)
   In a rocket ship (in a rocket ship),
   'Cause a rocket ship ('cause a rocket ship)
   Won't make the trip (won't make the trip).
   Oh, you'll never get to heaven in a rocket ship
   'Cause a rocket ship won't make the trip.
   I ain't a gonna grieve my Lord no more.

3. Oh, you'll never get to heaven (Oh, you'll never get to heaven)
   On an old tram car (on an old tram car),
   'Cause an old tram car ('cause an old tram car)
   Won't get that far (won't get that far).
   Oh, you'll never get to heaven in an old tram car
   'Cause an old tram car won't get that far.
   I ain't a gonna grieve my Lord no more.

4. Oh, you'll never get to heaven (Oh, you'll never get to heaven)
   With Superman (with Superman),
   'Cause the Lord, He is ('cause the Lord, He is)
   A Batman fan (a Batman fan).
   Oh, you'll never get to heaven with Superman
   'Cause the Lord, He is a Batman fan.
   I ain't a gonna grieve my Lord no more.

5. Oh, you'll never get to heaven (Oh, you'll never get to heaven)
   In a limousine (in a limousine)
   'Cause the Lord don't sell ('cause the Lord don't sell)
   No gasoline (no gasoline).
   Oh, you'll never get to heaven in a limousine
   'Cause the Lord don't sell no gasoline.
   I ain't a gonna grieve my Lord no more.

Yankee Doodle

Traditional

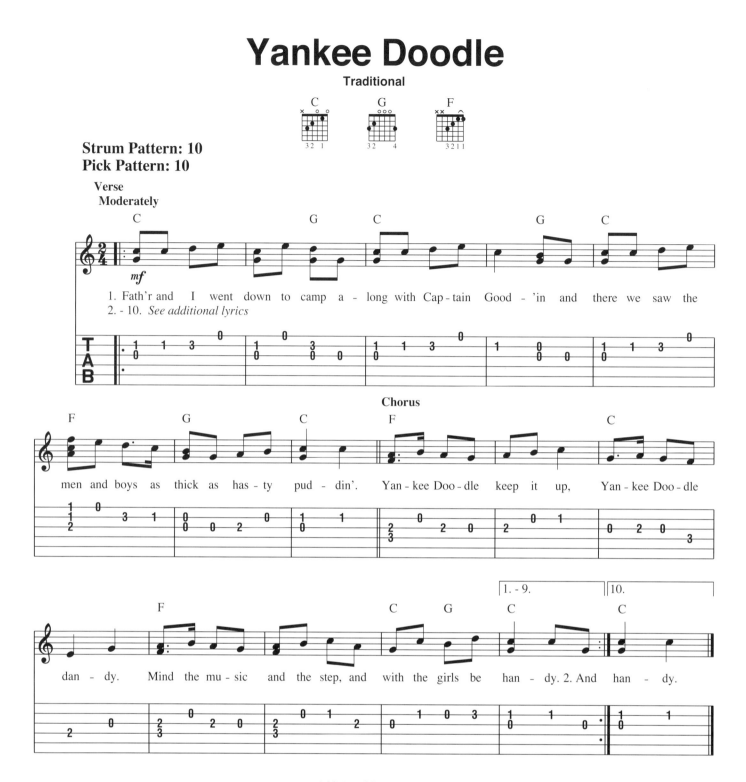

Strum Pattern: 10
Pick Pattern: 10

Additional Lyrics

2. And there we see a thousand men
   As rich as Squire David.
   And what they wasted ev'ry day
   I wish it could be saved.

3. And there was Captain Washington
   Upon a slapping stallion
   A-giving orders to his men,
   I guess there was a million.

4. And then the feathers on his hat,
   They looked so very fine, ah!
   I wanted peskily to get
   To give to my Jemima.

5. And there I see a swamping gun,
   Large as a log of maple,
   Upon a mighty little cart,
   A load for father's cattle.

6. And ev'ry time they fired it off,
   It took a horn of powder.
   It made a noise like father's gun,
   Only a nation louder.

7. An' there I see a little keg,
   Its head all made of leather.
   They knocked upon't with little sticks
   To call the folks together.

8. And Cap'n Davis had a gun,
   He kind o'clapt his hand on't
   And stuck a crooked stabbing-iron
   Upon the little end on't.

9. The troopers, too, would gallop up
   And fire right in our faces.
   It scared me almost half to death
   To see them run such races.

10. It scared me so I hooked it off
    Nor stopped, as I remember,
    Nor turned about till I got home,
    Locked up in mother's chamber.